Valentinus Basilius, Theodor Kerckring

Basil Valentine

His Triumphant Chariot of Antimony. With annotations of Theodore Kirkringius,

M.D.: with, The true book of the learned Synesius, a Greek abbot, taken out of the

Emperour's library, concerning the philosopher's stone

Valentinus Basilius, Theodor Kerckring

Basil Valentine
*His Triumphant Chariot of Antimony. With annotations of Theodore Kirkringius, M.D.: with,
The true book of the learned Synesius, a Greek abbot, taken out of the Emperour's library,
concerning the philosopher's stone*

ISBN/EAN: 9783337309367

Printed in Europe, USA, Canada, Australia, Japan

Cover: Foto ©Thomas Meinert / pixelio.de

More available books at **www.hansebooks.com**

BASIL VALENTINE

HIS

Triumphant Chariot

OF

ANTIMONY,

WITH

ANNOTATIONS

OF

Theodore Kirkringius. M. D.

WITH

The True Book' of the Learned *Synefius* a
Greek Abbot taken out of the Emperour's
Library, concerning the Philofopher's
Stone.

LONDON.

Printed for *Dorman Newman* at the Kings Arms
in the *Poultry.* 1678.

TO THE
READER.

IT is well known, that the prefent Subject, on which this eminent Author fo elegantly difcourfeth, was not long fince generally (though moft injurioufly) branded with the deteftable Name of Poyfon. This *Odium* was caft upon it (as appears by the prefent Book) in the Dayes of the Author; and perhaps, long before that time it might, through the Malice of idle Speculators, be condemned. For thofe Men, who prefume to be Mafters of all Knowledge, becaufe Letter-learned in the Theory of this or that Art, without the leaft Skill or Will to exercife themfelves in the Practice thereof, muft needs

con-

condemn what they do not underftand. And this they are induced
to do, left by approving what they
have no Knowledge of, they fhould
too palpably difcover their Ignorance; becaufe not able to evince
the Reafons of their own Approba-
tions. Therefore, 'tis too too probable, that they, hating Labour, and
envying the fedulous Endeavours of
others, left thereby their own
feeming Honour fhould be eclipfed,
would rather (according to the
Old Proverb) give *Antimony* an ill
Name, then foul their Hands in experiencing the Virtues, with which
it is endued. How ill it hath been
fpoken of in this our Time, is well
known to many; and of how fervice-
able ufe it hath been, in the Cure
of very many deplorable Difcafes,
within twenty years laft paft, is as
well underftood by moft of the in-
duftrioufly laborious Phyficians of
this City; who can, and dayly do,
when-

whenfoever they meet with Men of
like Induftry, teftify for the Author,
that unto *ANTIMONY* is not
undefervedly affigned a *C H A R I-
O T TRIVMPHANT.* For
none were permitted to enter *Rome*
in a Triumphant Chariot, that had
not flayn at leaft five thoufand *Enemies,* and obtained an intire Victory.
Wherefore, if *Antimony* (through
the Gift of the *moft* H I G H infited
in it) more than any one Simple of
Nature, be able to fubdue and expel
infinite Difeafes (the Enemies of
Humane Life) as is undoubtedly
known it is, and to obtain an intire
Victory over them, why fhould any
Man envy that, by which his own,
or his Neighbours, Life is or may be
fo well preferved? It is true, if taken
without Preparation or being ill
prepared (becaufe of the much E-
vil mixt with its great Good) 'tis
more injurious than profitable to
the Humane Body; which our Au-

A 3 thor

To the Reader.

thor well obferves, teaching fo many and laudable Preparations of the fame. Which Preparations are in no fmall Meafure illuftrated by the prefent Annotations of the Learned *Kirkringius*. Therefore the end of tranflating anew, and reprinting this Work now a fecond time in the Englifh Tongue, was partly becaufe of the aforefaid Annotations; and partly that fo Laudable a Work might not be obliterated by time, and by that means the pious and good Intentions of the Author be fruftrated, but wore efpecially, that our Ingenious Country Men, intent on the Knowledge of Natural things, might in their own native Language find whafoever is needful and neceffary for accomplifhing them in the Laudable Studies of the Works of Nature; without being neceffitated to feek forreign Aids, as many heretofore have been conftrained to do : be-

caufe

To the Reader.

caufe what they defired to be informed in, was lockt up in other Languages, and could not be unlocked,
but by few; who if able, were not
alwayes willing fo to do; and if
not able, though willing, could not
effect the fame.

For this very End, are the Works
of *Geber* the famous Arabian Prince,
and Philofopher, now likewife
tranflated into Fnglifh, ready for
the Prefs, and will be fpeedily pub-
lifhed. In the mean while, com-
mitting all to *G O D*, we heartily
wifh well to all, and to every Ingenious Student in the Practice of Chymical Phyfick good Succefs. Farewel.

The

THE
TABLE
OF
PARTICULARS
.Comprifed in the
WORKS
OF
BASIL VALENTINE.

A

Its

The Table.

The Table.

Of

The Table.

Of

The Table.

Ans-

The Table.

Prepa-

The Table.

ERRATA

PAge. 4. line. 32. read *Graces.* p. 21. l. 11. r. *Midas.* p. 33. l. 12. r. *him.* p. 37. l. 14. r. *into it.* p. 68. l. last, r. *force.* p. 77. l. 8. r. *will not.* p. 90. l. 16. r. *commodiously.* p. 94. l. 3. add *not.* p. 107. l. 36. r. *on it.* p. 109. l. 35. add *in.* p. ibid. l. 22. dele *again.* p. 124. l. 25. dele *of Wine.* p. 125. l. 20. r. *Prayse.* p. 127. l. 15. r. *Extraction.* p. 129. l. 5. add, *you.* 134. l. 4. r. *his.* p. 156. l. 7. r. *Precipitate.*

BASIL

BASIL VALENTINE

HIS

Triumphant Chariot

OF

ANTIMONY.

Since I, *Bafil Valentine*, by Religious Vows am bound to live according to the Order of St. *Benedict*, and that requires another manner of Spirit of Holinefs, then the common State of Mortals exercifed in the prophane bufinefs of this World; I thought it my duty before all things, in the beginning of this little Book, to declare what is neceffary to be known by the pious *Spagyrift*, inflamed with an ardent defire of this *Art*; as, what he ought to do, and whereunto to direct his aim, that he may lay fuch Foundations of the whole matter, as may be ftable; left his Building fhaken with Winds, happen to fail, and the whole Edifice to be involved in fhameful Ruine, which otherwife, being founded on more firm and folid Principles, might have continued for a long feries of time. Which Admonition I judged was, is, and always will be a neceffary part of my Religious Office; efpecially, fince we muft all die, and no one of us, which now are, whether high or low, fhall

B   long

long be ſeen among the number of Men. For it concerns me to commend theſe Meditations of Mortality to Poſterity, leaving them behind me, not only that honour may be given to the Divine Majeſty, but alſo that Men may obey him ſincerely in all things.

In this my Meditation I found that there were five principal Heads, chiefly to be conſidered by the wiſe and prudent Spectators of our Wiſdom and Art. The firſt of which is, *Invocation* of *GOD*. The ſecond, *Contemplation* of *Nature*. The third, *True Preparation*. The fourth, The *Way* of *Uſing*. The fifth, *Utility* and *Fruit*. For he, who regards not theſe, ſhall never obtain place among true *Chymiſts*, or fill up the number of perfect *Spagyriſts*. Therefore touching theſe five Heads we ſhall here following treat, and ſo far declare them, as that the general Work may be brought to light and perfected by an intent and ſtudious Operator.

1. *Invocation* of *GOD* muſt be made with a certain Heavenly Intention, drawn from the bottom of a pure and ſincere Heart, and Conſcience, free from all Ambition, Hypocriſie, and all other Vices, which have any affinity with theſe, as Arrogancy, Boldneſs, Pride, Luxury, Mundane Petulancy, Oppreſſion of the Poor, and other dependent evils, all which are to be eradicated out of the Heart; that when a Man deſires to proſtrate himſelf before the Throne of Grace, for obtaining bodily health, he may do that with a Conſcience free from all unprofitable Weeds, that his Body may be tranſmuted into an Holy Temple of *GOD*, and be purged from every uncleanneſs. For *GOD* will not be mocked (which I earneſtly admoniſh) as Worldly Men, pleaſing and flattering themſelves with their own Wiſdom, think: *GOD*, I ſay, will not be mocked, but the Creator of all things will be invoked with re-

verential

verential fear, and acknowledged with due Obedidience. And for this there is great Reafon. For what hath Man, that he muft not own to be received from this his Omnipotent Creator, whether you have refpect to the Body, or to the Soul, which operates in the Body? Hath not he, for fuftentation of this, out of his meer Mercy communicated to us his Eternal *WORD*, and alfo promifed Eternal *Salvation*? Hath not he alfo provided food and cloathing for the Body, and all thofe things, without which the Body cannot fubfift? All thefe, by humble Prayer a Man obtains of that moft excellent Father, who created Heaven and Earth, together with things Vifible and Invifible, as the Firmament, Elements, Vegetables, and Animals. Which is fo very true, that I am certainly affured, no Impious Man fhall ever be partaker of true Medicine, much lefs of the Eternal Heavenly Bread. Therefore place your whole Intention and Truft in *GOD*, call upon him and pray, that he may impart his bleffing to you: let this be the beginning of your Work, that by the fame you may obtain your defired end, and at length effect what you intended. *For the Fear of the Lord is the beginning of Wifdom.*

Whofoever purpofeth in himfelf to feek after that, which is the greateft of Terrene things, efpecially the knowledge of every good thing, that is in the Creatures, and *GOD* hath liberally imparted to Men, and implanted (as to their effective power) in *Stones, Herbs, Roots, Seeds, Animals, Plants, Minerals, Metals,* yea and indeed in all things; let him caft away all Earthly thoughts, reject all that depends on them, and hope for freenefs of Heart, and pray unto *GOD* with great lowlynefs of mind: So doing, his hope of freenefs may at length be turned into true freedom. Which no Man will doubt, who knows, that he alone is *GOD*, who de-

livered *Ifrael* from all his Enemies; which delive-
rance he did in very deed effect, not only for *Ifrael;*
but alfo for all Men making humble fupplications
to him, and praying with brokennefs of Heart.
Therefore let Prayer be the firft point of our Admonition, which alfo is, and by us is called *Invocation* of *GOD*, which if made, not with Hypocrifie
and a feigned Heart, but with fuch Faith and Truft,
as that, with which the *Centurion* in *Capernaum* prayed; with fuch lowlinefs of mind, and confeffion of
Sins, as the *Woman* of *Canaan* was endued with; with
fuch Charity as the *Samaritan* fhewed to the Man
wounded in the Way to *Jericho*, pouring Wine and
Oyl into his Wounds, paying his Charges in the
Inn, and giving order he fhould be very carefully
looked to; Laftly, if a Man's Chriftian Charity ex-
tends it felf fo far, as if he obtain what he prays
for, he would willingly communicate of the fame
to his Neighbour, then he fhall undoubtedly obtain Riches and Health, the end of his *Prayer.* *

* *What the Author hath premifed here at large, and elfewhere often inferted
touching* Piety, *the Worfhip of* GOD, *and Invocation of his Name, I purpofe
neither to praife nor difpraife; Let them be judged figns of his own earneft
Piety, Arguments of his fincerity, and fignate Impreffes of his fervent zeal (by
fo many Tautologies and Reiterations) often boiling up. Every Man, according
to the Opinion of his mind, and the perfwafion, in which he was educated from
his childhood, will more or lefs efteem of this. It was my bufinefs to tranflate
the Authors writings into Latin, in fuch a Method and Order, as I thought
would in no wife give any diftafte to the delicate Palat of the Reader; alfo
to indicate that, which feems pertinent to the bufinefs of every Chymift and true
Spagyrift, and not to neglect the other. For fince Piety is available for all
things, as divine Oracles teach, and the principal exercife of Piety is Prayer;
by which Celeftial Gifts are obtained of GOD the giver of all good things;
our Author wills, that unto him the mind be lifted up, even in the midft of the
Operations of Chymiftry full of labour and toil. If Prayer effected no other
thing, it certainly collects the mind (called away from all other things) into it
felf and renders it apt for that, which is in hand; whence it comes to pafs,
that it reflects upon many things, and confiders them, which otherwife would
not enter the mind, if it fet about its work perjunctorily, and diftracted with*

various Conceptions: And so, by the help of Prayer *we receive many things, which we (if not ungrateful) must needs acknowledge we have obtained from* GOD. *How often this is found to be of use in* Spagyrick Works *every Man knows, that hath any time intirely devoted himself to this business ; viz. how often those things which he long sought and could not find, have been imparted to him in a moment, and as it were infused from above, or dictated by some good* Genius. *That also is of use in dissolving all* Riddles *, or Ænigmatical writings : For if you burn with a great desire of knowing them, that is* Prayer *; and when you incline your mind to this or that, variously discussing and meditating many things, this is* Co-operation *; that your* Prayer *may not be idle, or tempting* GOD *: yet this your endeavour is in vain, until you find the Solution. Nevertheless if you despair not, but instantly persist in desire, and cease not from labour, at length in a moment the* Solution *will fall in ; this is* Revelation, *which you cannot receive unless you pray with great desire and labour, using your utmost endeavour ; and yet you cannot perceive, how from all those things (of which you thought) which were not the* Solution *of the Ænigma, the* Solution *it self arose. This unfolding of the* Riddle *opens to you the mystery of all great things, and shews how available* Prayer *is for the obtaining of things Spiritual and Eternal, as well as Corporal and perishing goods : and when* Prayer *is made with a Heart not feigned, but sincere; you will see that there is nothing more fit for the acquiring of what you desire. Let these suffice to be spoken of* Prayer, *which* Basilius *and all* Philosophers *with him do not vainly require, as an Introduction to* Chymistry. *For* Piety *is profitable for all works, especially for all* Great Undertakings.

2. Next in order after *Prayer* is *Contemplation*, by which I understand an accurate attention to the business it self, under which will fall these considerations first to be noted. As, what are the *Circumstances* of any thing, what the *Matter*, what the *Form*, whence its Operations proceed , whence it is infused and implanted, how generated by the *Stars*, conformed by the *Elements* , produced and perfected by the three *Principles*. Also how the body of every thing may be dissolved, that is, resolved into the first *Matter*, or first *Essence* (of which I have already made mention in other of my writings) *viz.* how the last Matter may be changed into the first, and the first into the last. *

* *What are here set down, touching the true* Theory *of* Philosophy, *are*

This

Compendiums of thoſe things, which Philoſophers *have in ſo many Books (writ about the ſame buſineſs) revealed, ſhall I ſay, or concealed. Attend to the words of the* Authour, *and you will ſee, that he perfectly knew that* Spirit *penetrating all things, which preſides or bears rule in all things, yet is involved and abſconded in matter and defilements on every ſide; from which if once freed, it returns to the purity of its own ſubſtance, in which it produceth all things, and is all in all. To comment upon this, would be a work no leſs than the produducing of all* Books *of* Philoſophers, *compiled with ſuch accurate ſtudy, and contending with ſo great contention about the* Theory.

This *Contemplation*, which abſolves the ſecond part of our Admonition, is Celeſtial, and to be underſtood with Spiritual Reaſon; for the circumſtances and depth of every thing cannot be perceived any other way, then by the Spiritual cogitation of Man: and this *Contemplation* is twofold. One is called poſſible, the other impoſſible. The later conſiſts in copious cogitations, which never proceed to effects, nor exhibit any form of a matter, which falls under the Touch. As if any one ſhould endeavour to comprehend the Eternity of the Moſt High, which is vain and impoſſible, yea a Sin againſt the Holy Spirit, ſo arrogantly to pry into the *Divinity* it ſelf, which is Immenſe, Infinite, and Eternal; and to ſubject the incomprehenſive Counſel of the Secrets of *GOD*, to humane Inquiſition. The other part of *Contemplation*, which is poſſible, is called the *Theory*. This contemplates that, which is perceived by Touch and Sight, and hath a formed *Nature* in time: this conſiders, how that nature may be helped and perfected by Reſolution of it ſelf; how every body may give forth from it ſelf, the good or evil, Venome or Medicine latent in it; how Deſtruction and Confraction are to be handled, whereby under a juſt Title, without Sophiſtical deceits, the pure may be ſevered and ſeparated from the impure. This *Separation* is inſtituted and made by divers manual operations, and various

various ways; Some of which are vulgarly known by experience, others remote from vulgar experience. These are, *Calcination, Sublimation, Reverberation, Circulation, Putrefaction, Digestion, Distillation, Cohobation, Fixation*, and the like of these; all the degrees of which are found in operating, learned, perceived and manifested by the same. Whence clearly appears what is moveable, what is fixed, what is white, red, black, blew, or green, *viz.* when the operation is rightly instituted by the Artificer, for possibly the Operator may err, and turn aside from the right way; but that *Nature* should err, when rightly handled, is not possible. Therefore if you shall err, so that *Nature* cannot be altogether free, and released from the Body, in which it is held Captive, return again into your way, learn the *Theory* more perfectly, and enquire more accurately in the method of operating, that you may find the foundation and certainty in Separation of all things. Which is a matter of great concern. And this is the second foundation of Philosophy, which follows *Prayer* : for in that the sum of the matter lies, and is contained in these words. Seek first the *Kingdom* of *GOD*, and his *Justice* by *Prayer*, and all other things, which Man seeks in these Temporals, and he hath need of, either for the sustentation or health of his body, shall be added to you.

3. Next to the *Theory*, which searcheth out the inmost properties of things, follows *Preparation*, which is performed by Operation of the hands, that some real work may be produced. From *Preparation* ariseth Knowledge, *viz.* Such, as opens all the fundamentals of Medicine. Operation of the Hands requires a diligent application of it self, but the praise of Science consists in experience, but the difference of these *Anatomy* distinguish-

guiſheth, * Operation ſhews how all things may be brought to light, and expoſed to ſight viſibly: but knowledge ſhews the practice; and that, whence the true Practitioner is, and is no other then confirmation: becauſe the operation of the hands manifeſts ſomething that is good, and draws the latent and hidden nature outwards, and brings it to light for good. For, as in Spirituals, the way of the Lord is to be prepared; ſo alſo in theſe things, the way is to be opened and prepared, that no errour be from the right path, and Proceſs may be made, without devious errours, in the direct way to health.

---

* *Manual Operation is chiefly required in this third Part, without which, every Operation, like a Ship wanting Ballaſt, floats and is uncertain. It is difficult to expreſs this with a Pen; for more is learned by once ſeeing the work done, then can be taught by the writing of many Pages; yet if it be no offence to you, to peruſe theſe* Commentaries *together with* Baſilius *(in this ſo neceſſary part) will not a little help.*

4. After *Preparation*, and eſpecially after ſeparation of the good from the evil, we are to proceed to the * *Uſe* of the Weight or doſe, that neither more, nor leſs then is fit, may be given. For above all things, the Phyſician ought well to know, whether his Medicament will be weak or ſtrong, alſo whether it will do good, or hurt, unleſs he reſolve to fatten the Church-yard, with the loſs of his fame, and hazard of his own Soul.

---

* *By* Uſe, *the Author underſtands what others call* Doſe; *for what will a good Medicine profit you, if you know not in what quantity to adminiſter it; that the ſame may rather heal, then hurt or kill. By experience only to learn this, is a work full of perilous caſualty, yet the Diſcipline or knowledge of Doſes was found out this way firſt, and afterward eaſily taught by words. Where a living Voice is wanting, it is ſafer to be too timerous, then in any wiſe bold or adventurous, although of Antimony I can affirm, that being duly prepared it is as harmleſs a Medicine as* Caſſia *or* Manna. *The whole caution is*

chiefly about its use, after the first preparations ; because it may still retain much of its own crude Venome.

5. After the Medicament is taken into the body, and hath diffused it self through all the Members, that it may search out those defects against which it was administred, the *Utility* comes to be considered; for it is possible, that a Medicament diligently prepared, and exhibited in due weight, may do more hurt then good in some Diseases, and seem to be Venome rather then Medicine. Hence an accurate reflexion is to be made to those things, which profit or help; and they are diligently to be noted, that we may be mindful to observe the same in other cases.

Yet both in the * *Use* and *Utility*, this one thing is necessary to be considered, *viz.* whether the Disease be an external and open wound, or only an internal and latent evil: for as the difference of these is great, so the way of curation is not the same. Therefore the bottom of every Disease is to be known, that it may be understood, whether the same may be cured by external remedies only, or must from within be driven outwards.

* *That Indication is to be taken from things helping and hurting, is known even to Tyro's. But what the Authour subjoyns touching internal and external curation, are not so rude, as not to deserve good Attention: And also those things which he permixeth with his own Satyrical Reprehension, if the Reader be so wise as to believe that Basilius intermixed them to deter the unworthy deriders of Chymistry from approaching to his sacred Arcanums, he will be wise for himself. For whilst others rail and swell with indignation, he gathers the fruit of the Authour's Axioms, which as another Agent he scattered among these Thorns. Whilst you, O lover of Chymistry, peruse these, so long will I keep silence.*

For if the Center of the Disease be within, such a Medicine must be given, as can search out, apprehend and restore that Center: otherwise the

Physi-

Phyfician's labour will be fruitlefs and in vain.

Moreover, if there be an internal Difeafe, which arifeth, and is fed from an internal Original, it muft never be driven inward by external remedies; for great difcommodity will thence enfue, and at length Death it felf. Which may be underftood by the fimilitude of a Tree: for if any one, whilft it germinates or flowers, repels the Humours to the Interiours, whence they proceeded to the nutriment of the Earth; that Tree will be fo far from bringing forth the defired Fruit by the flower, that a fuffocation of the fame arifeth from the violent conjunction of humours not finding any out-let. Therefore there is great difference between frefh wounds inflicted by Prick, Cut, or any other way, and the old which derive their Original from within. For the frefh wounds may be perfectly cured by external remedies only; but in thofe, which are nourifhed from within, an external application of Oyls, Balfoms, Unguents, and Plaifters profits little, unlefs the Internal Fountain be ftopped, whence the humours flow to the external parts. When the Fountain fhall be ftopped, the Flux will ceafe, and the evil may eafily be cured with Diet only. It is no great point of Art to heal any frefh wound; for this every Country-man can eafily effect with crude Lard: but to remove all Symptomes which happen in wounds, and to dry up the Fountain of the evil, this is the work, and this the labour of the Artift.

Now come hither, you Phyficians, how many foever there be of you, that arrogate to your felves the Title of Doctor of either Medicine, *viz.* of internal and external Difeafes; underftand ye the Title of your honour, and confult your own Confcience, and fee, whether you received that from *GOD*, that is, poffefs it in verity, or whether you ufurp it as a form, for honour fake. For, as much

as

as Heaven is diſtant from the Earth, ſo vaſtly different is the Art of healing internal Diſeaſes, from
the Sanation of external wounds. If the Title be
given to you by *GOD*, the ſame *GOD* will give a
Bleſſing, Felicity, Health, and happy events; but if
your Title be vain, and only deviſed and aſſumed
for ambition, all things will evilly ſucceed to you:
your honour will fail, and you will prepare for your
ſelf Hell-fire, which can no more be extinguiſhed,
then it can be expreſſed by words. For Chriſt ſaid
to his Diſciples; *You call me Lord and Maſter, and*
ye do well, Therefore whoſoever aſſumes a Title
of Honour, let him ſee, whether he do well, and
whether he aſcribes not more to himſelf, than he
knows and hath learned, which is the real abuſe of
this Title. For he, who will write himſelf Doctor
of either Medicine, ought to underſtand, know,
and be well skilled in both, *viz.* the Internal and
External Medicine. Nor ſhould he be ignorant of
Anatomy, that he may be able to ſhew the Conſtitu-
tion of the Body, and diſcover from what Member
every Diſeaſe proceeds, together with its Fountain
and cauſe. Alſo remedies, with which he may cure
the Diſeaſe, and circumſtances of external Wounds,
are to be underſtood by him. Good *GOD*! where
will the Title be found, what will become of the
Maſter, when an exact Trial ſhall be made, for dif-
covering the ignorance of theſe *Doctors* of either
Medicine?

In times paſt, long before my days, the Doctors
of Medicine did themſelves cure External wounds,
and judged that a part of their Office; but in theſe
our times, they take Servants, whom they employ
in theſe things, and this way the nobleſt of Arts is
become a Mechanick Operation; and ſome of thoſe
who exerciſe it, are indeed ſo very rude, as they
know not Letters, and ſcarcely know how (according

ing to the Proverb) to drive an Aſs out of the Corn.
Theſe, I ſay, profeſs themſelves Maſters in curing
wounds, and Doctors of Doctors; and to ſpeak the
truth as it is, they may by a better right glory in
this Title, then thou magnificent Doctor, umbrati-
cal Chyrurgion, and moſt ignorant Boaſter of Ti-
tles, why do you ſtile your ſelf Doctor of either
Medicine.　What more now Maſter Doctor, what
ſay you, moſt expert Chyrurgion? I pray be not
offended at this, or take it amiſs; for you your ſelf
will quickly confeſs, if you do but ſeriouſly conſider
wounds made by Prick or Cut, that you have as
much knowledge in the cure of them, as is in the
Brain of a dunghil Cock, which Children learning
their A. B. C. are wont to ſet in the Frontiſpiece of
their Primer.

Therefore I perſwade all Men, of what ſtate or
condition ſoever, who are deſirous of Learning,
from your Maſters to ſearch out the true Doctrine,
which conſiſts in *Preparation*, and afterward in the
Uſe; ſo they, or you, ſhall poſſeſs the Title aſſumed
with honour, and Men will undoubtedly have confidence in you, and you will in very deed do them
good, then will you to the Eternal Creator give
thanks cordially without feigning.　But let every
Man ſeriouſly think with himſelf, what it is he
ought to do, and what he is to omit, and whether
he doth juſtly or unjuſtly uſe the Title aſſumed.
For he, who aſſumes any Title, ought eſpecially to
underſtand the condition of that Title, and why
he aſſumed it, or what the true foundation is.　It
is not ſufficient, if any one with the vulgar ſay (ſa-
ving your reverence, let the more delicate Men
pardon us, if we intending to ſpeak to the purpoſe,
make mention of putrefaction) this is egregious
dung, it hath a ſtrong and grievous ill ſavour, and
know not how it comes to paſs, that a Man, who
perhaps

perhaps eats food of a most grateful taste and o-
dour, and well accommodated to his natural Appetite, thence makes excrement endued with qualities so contrary, and yielding an odour so very un-
grateful, and repugnant to Nature : of which there
is no other reason, then natural putrefaction and
corruption. The same happens in all Aromatical
well smelling things. It is the Philosophers part
to enquire, what odour is, and whence it receives
its vertues, and in what the virtue of it may be
made manifest to true profit. For the Earth is
nourished and fatned by stinking dung, and noble
Fruit is produced of it. Of this matter there is
not one cause only, but our Book would swell to an
huge Volume, if we should but briefly hint at all
natural Generations and mutations; yet *Digestion*
and *Putrefaction* are the principal keys of them.
For the *Fire* and *Air* make a certain *Maturation*, by
which a Transmutation of the *Earth* and *Water* may
follow; and this is also a certain mutation, by which
of evil smelling Dung a most fragrant Balsam may
be produced; and on the contrary, of most grateful Balsam ill savoured Dung. But perhaps you
will say, why do I produce examples so very rude
and absurd? I do confess the example is taken from
a Cottage, rather then a Royal Court; yet a prudent considerer of things, more accurately diving
into the matter, will easily understand, what such
examples intimate to him, *viz.* that of the highest
things the lowest are made, and of the lowest the
highest, so that, of a Medicament is produced Venome, and of Venome Medicine; of the sweet,
bitter, acid, and corrosive; and on the contrary
of the corrosive, another thing more profitable.

O good *GOD*, how much is Nature absconded
from Men, so that she seems to disdain to be wholly
seen by us? But since thou hast ordained so very
                                          short

fhort a time of our Life, and thou the Judge of all,
referveft many things to thy felf in the Creatures,
which thou haft left to be admired, not known, by
us, and of which thou alone wilt be the beholder
and Judge, grant unto me, that unto my Life's end
I may keep thee and my Saviour in my Heart, that
befides health and neceffaries of the Body, which
thou haft liberally beftowed, I may alfo acquire the
health of my Soul and Spiritual Riches; of which
ineftimable good I am freed from all doubt by that
thy mercy, in which, for me a miferable finner,
thou didft (on the Tree of the Crofs) fhed the Sulphur and Balfom of my Soul; which is indeed a
mortiferous Venome to the Devil, but to us Sinners
a moft prefent remedy. I do certainly heal my
Brethren, as far as concerns the Soul, by Prayer, and
in relation to the body, with apt Remedies; therefore I hope they will on their parts ufe their endeavour, that they with me, and I with them, may at
length inhabit the Tabernacle of the Moft High,
and in him our *GOD* enjoy Eternity.

But to return to my Philofophy of *Antimony*, I
would have the Reader, before all other things, to
underftand, that all things contain in themfelves
operative and vivificative Spirits; which inhabi-
ting in the Body feed and nourifh themfelves, and
are fuftained by the Body. Elements themfelves
want not thefe Spirits, which (the living *GOD* per-
mitting that) whether they be good or evil, have
their Habitation in them. Men and Animals have
in them a living operating Spirit, which receding
from them, nothing but a Carkafs remains. In
Herbs, and all things bearing Fruit, a Spirit of Sanity exifts; otherwife they could not, by any Preparation, be reduced to Medicinal ufe. Metals and
all Minerals, are endued and poffeffed with their
own incomprehenfible Spirit, in which, the power
and

and virtue of all their poſſible effects, conſiſts. For whatſoever is without Spirit, wants Life, and contains in it ſelf no vivifying Virtue. Therefore, you are to know, that in *Antimony* alſo there is a Spirit, which effects whatſoever is in it, or can proceed from it, in an inviſible way and manner, no otherwiſe, than as in the *Magnet* is abſconded a certain inviſible power, as we ſhall more largely treat in its own place, where we ſpeak of the *Magnet*.

But there are various kinds of Spirits; * viſible to the Intellect, and endued with Spiritual knowledge, which notwithſtanding cannot (when they will) be touched or apprehended, as Natural Men are touched; eſpecially they, who have their fixed Reſidence in Elements, as are the Spirits of Fire, Lights, and other Objects formally darting out Light from themſelves: ſuch are *Airy* Spirits, who inhabit the Air; *Aqueous* Spirits living in Waters; and *Terrene* Spirits living in the Earth, which we Men call *Earthly Men*, which are chiefly found in wealthy Mines of the Earth, where they ſhew and diſcover themſelves to us.

* *what follow, ſeem ſomewhat confuſed; according to the Sentiments of certain* Theologicians, *who have held various opinions of Spirits reſiding in the Fire, Air, and other Elements; adjudging them to the Eternal Fire of Hell,&c. All which with* Baſilius, *we leave as unknown, to the Judgement of the Divine Knowledge. But what he himſelf ſubjoyns, touching the wonderful virtue and power of Antimonial and all other Chymical Spirits, which we our ſelves with ſo great admiration have often ſeen, we underſtand only of material Spirits; which certainly are endued with as great virtues, and effect things no leſs wonderful then thoſe Spirits, which phantaſtick perſons (oppreſſed with Melancholy) affirm they ſee and talk with; yea I cannot remember that I ever found written or declared (by ſuch, as taking a liberty of lying, endeavour to pleaſe or terrifie others) any greater or more wonderful virtues then theſe Spirits have.*

Theſe Spirits are endued with Senſes and Underſtanding, know Arts, and can change themſelves
into

into divers Forms, until the time of their Judgement; but whether a definitory ſentence ought to be pronounced againſt them as yet, or no, that I leave to the Providence of the Divine Majeſty, from whom nothing is hid. There are other Spirits, wanting ſpeech, which cannot ſhew themſelves viſibly in the very act; and they are thoſe which live in Animals, as in Men and the like, in Plants alſo and in Minerals; neverthelefs they have in themſelves an occult and operative Life, and manifeſt and diſcover themſelves by their efficacious power of operating, which they contain in and bear about themſelves, and moſt apparently give teſtimony of their virtue of healing, whenſoever that (by the help of Art) is extracted from them, being accurately ſeparated from their body. After the ſame manner, the efficacious Spirit, and operative power of *Antimony*, manifeſts its gifts, and diſtributes them among Men, being firſt looſed from its own body, and freed from all its bonds, ſo, that it is able to penetrate, and rendred fit to be applyed to thoſe Uſes, which the Artificer propoſed to himſelf in Preparation.

But the Artiſt and *Vulcan* ought to agree: the Fire gives ſeparation for an operative power, and the Artificer forms the matter. As a Black-ſmith uſeth one ſort of Fire, alſo Iron only is his matter, which he intends for forming divers Inſtruments. For ſome times of it he makes a Spit, at another time Horſe-ſhoes, another time a Saw, and at length innumerable other things, every of which ſerves for that Uſe, unto which the Smith intended it, although the matter is but one, which he prepares for ſo many divers uſes. So of *Antimony* various works may be made for different uſes: in which the Artiſt is the Smith that forms; *Vulcan* is as it were the key which opers; and Operation and Utility

tility give experience, and knowledge of the Ufe.
O! if foolifh and vain Men had but Ears to hear,
and true eyes with underftanding, not only for hearing what I write, but for underftanding the *Arcanum* and knowledge of the ufe; affuredly they
would not fuck in thofe infalubrious and turbid Po-
tions, but haften to thefe limped Fountains, and
drink of the Well of Life.

Therefore let the World know, that I fhall
prove thofe pretended Doctors, who feem to be
wife, to be mere Fools and Idebts, and caufe many
unlearned Men (but fuch as are ftudious Difciples of
my Doctrine) to become true Doctors in very deed.
Wherefore I here folemnly cite and invite all Men,
who earneftly afpire to knowledge, with a chearful
mind, good Confcience, and certain hope, to em-
brace and become Spectators of our Doctrine, and
accurately to perufe my Writings and Informations;
for fo, at length, they (being poffeffors of what
they fought) will extol and commend me after
death, rendring my mortal fame immortal, with
their perpetual remembrance of my praifes, as
long as the World endures. But if when I am
dead, any one be pleafed to inftitute a difputation
in the Schools againft me, my writings will fully
anfwer all his Objections, and I am affured my Difciples will never forget the benefit received from
me, by which they will obtain the Empire of Truth;
which ever was to me, and always will be to them,
fufficient to fupprefs a Lie to the Worlds end.

Alfo let the well meaning and fincere obferver of
Art know, that there are two kinds of *Antimony*
very different each from other: one is fair, pure,
and of a golden property, and that contains very
much *Mercury*, but the other which hath much *Sulphur* is not fo friendly to gold as the firft, and is diftinguifhed by fair long and white fhining ftreaks.

C   There

Therefore one is more fit for Medicine and *Alchimy*, then the other: as when the Flefh of Fifhes is compared with the Flefh of other Animals, although both thefe are, and are called Flefh, yet each of thefe very much differs from the Flefh of the other; even fo of *Antimony* the difference is the fame. Many do indeed write of the Interiour virtue of *Antimony*, but few of them ever taught the true Foundation of the virtues with which it is endued, or found out which way, or in what manner it receives them; So that their Doctrine is founded upon words only, exifts without any true foundation, and they themfelves lofe the Fruit they hoped to receive by fuch Writings. For to write truly of *Antimony* is a work that requires profound Meditations, a mind largely unfolding it felf, and knowledge of its manifold *Preparation*, and of the true *Soul* of it, in which all the Utility is cited, and which being known you may be able to give an indubitate Judgement, of what evil or good, Venome or Medicine is latent therein. It is not a matter of fmall moment by a true *Examen* to fearch into *Antimony*, and thereby to penetrate fundamentally into its Effence, and through earneft ftudy to attain the final knowledge thereof, that the Venenofity of the fame (againft which unskilful Men ignorantly exclaim) may be taken away, and it be changed and prepared into a better State, becoming a Medicine fit for ufe and void of Venome.

Many Artifts intending to Anatomize *Antimony*, have divers ways vexed, wrefted and tormented the fame, in fuch wife as it cannot be well defcribed in Words, much lefs believed; yet, the matter being truly examined, they effected nothing. For they fought not its true Soul, and therefore could not find the feigned Soul of it, which themfelves fought. By the black Colours a mift was caft before their

Eyes,

Eyes, fo that they could neither obferve the true Soul it felf, nor know it. For *Antimony* like unto *Mercury*, may fitly be compared to a round Circle, of which there is no end; in which the more diligently any Man feeks, the more he finds, if Procefs be made by him in a right way and due order. Yet the Life of no one Man is fufficient for him to learn all the myfteries thereof. It is Venome and a moft fwift poyfon, alfo it is void of Venome and a moft excellent Medicine; whether it be ufed outwardly or inwardly. Which is a thing hid from moft Men by reafon of their own blindnefs; and they judge it an incredible, foolifh and vain work, becaufe (through their ignorance) it is unknown to them, who can no otherwife be excufed, then that they deferve the name of Stupidity: yet that is not to be fuffered in them, becaufe they defire not to learn or be better informed, either here, or elfewhere.

Antimony is endued with all the four firft qualities; it is cold and humid, and again it is hot and dry, and accommodates it felf to the four Seafons of the year, alfo it is volatile and fixed: The volatile part of it is not void of Venome, but the fixed is free from all venenofity; which is fo very ftrange, as it may be reputed one of the feven Wonders of the World, of which fo many Writers have difcourfed, not knowing themfelves what they writ. There hath been no * Man before me, and at this day there is none found, who hath fo throughly learned the power, virtue, ftrength, operation, and efficacy of *Antimony*, or fo profoundly penetrated into all the *Energy* thereof, as nothing more is latent in it unfound out, or which cannot be brought to light by experience. If fuch a Man could be found he would be worthy to be carried about in a *Triumphant Chariot*, as in times paft was granted to Monarchs, and

potent

potent Heroes, after they had happily fought Battels, and were returned with Victory. But I fear, that many of our Doctors will be conftrained to provide a Chariot for themfelves.

* Here the Authour fpeaks largely in commendation of Antimony. *Read, read (I fay) O Lover of* Chymiftry, *and you will find nothing Hyperbolical, nor any thing Thrafonick.* Bafilius *in fpeaking as he doth, hath not exhaufted the Praifes of Antimony ; becaufe no Man unto this day could ever experience all its Virtues. We have feen many of its Effects, and many new Effects are daily found by curious Searchers, yet many more remain unknown. So that, as in Fire is an inexhauftible Fountain ; (for the more you take from it, the more it gives) fo in* Antimony *is an ineftimable Treafure of new Virtues. For if from it you extract its* Acetum *a thoufand times, it will a thoufand times yeild new* Acetum. *Nature feems to have made choyce of this Mineral, therein to hide all her Treafures. Therefore not without reafon hath* Bafilius *made for it a* Triumphant Chariot, *which is daily enriched with Spoyls taken from the Camps of Ignorance.*

For the Mafters of this terrene World are fo intangled with their own Thoughts, that they feek nothing from Antimony but Riches, and forget to fearch its utility for medicine, and the Health of the Body, which notwithftanding ought above all things to be fought, that (being brought to Light) the wonderful Works of our *GOD* may be made manifeft, and the Glory given to him, with great thankfulnefs. It is not to be denyed, but that more of Riches and Health may be found in it than either you all, or I my felf, can believe : for I profefs my felf no other than a Difciple in the Knowledge of Antimony, although in it I have feen, experienced, and learned more than you, and all fuch as you are (who arrogate to your felves great skill therein) either have learned, or ever can learn. Yet no Man fhould therefore be troubled, or defpair of his well doing, fince *GOD* wonderfully difpenfeth his Goods and Benefits; but becaufe the World, indulging their own Ingratitude, have neither efteemed, nor with due Reverence acknowledged the Munificence of the Moſt High, but have preferred Riches before Health, *GOD* hath ſpread as it were a Spider's Webb before their Eyes, that being blind they might not know the Secrets of Nature abſconded in the Form of this Mineral.

All men cry out Rich, Rich we would be. I confeſs you all aſpire to Riches, and with the Epicure ſay, *The Body muſt firſt be provided for, the Soul may at length alſo find ſomewhat*; and with *Midas* (as in the Fable) you deſire that all things whatſoever you touch may be turned into Gold. Hence it is, that ſo many ſeek their deſired Riches in *Antimony:* But becauſe they accept not that Guift of the Creator with a grateful Heart, which before all Things ſhould be procured, and caſt the Love of their Neighbour behind their back, therefore they in vain look the Horſe in the Mouth; for they know his Age and Strength no more than the Gueſts at the Marriage-Feaſt in *Cana* of *Galilee* knew the wonderful Work, which *Chriſt* there wrought, when he turned Water into Wine. They knew, that Wine was Water, and that the Water was turned into Wine, they perceived by the Taſt; but how that Tranſmutation happened was hid from them. For the Lord JESUS, our Saviour, reſerved that Supernatural Work to himſelf, as a Teſtimony of his Omnipotency. Wherefore I ſay, it is every Man's duty, to ſearch out the Myſteries and *Arcanums*, which the Creator hath inſired in all Creatures; for although (as we ſaid) it is not Credible, that we Men can throughly learn and penetrate all Things; yet we are not forbid to inquire into them, ſince by Study and Diligence ſo much may be effected, as although through ſome defect a Man be hindred in ſuch wiſe, as he cannot attain to the deſired Riches

and

and perfect Sanity, yet he may acquire enough to occasion him not to repent of his Labour, but rather to minister unto him matter of Joy and Rejoycing, that he sees himself so far an *Adeptist*, as he stands always obliged to render thanks to his *Creator*.

Therefore, whofoever defires to become a perfect Anatomist of *Antimony*, the firft thing to be confidered by him is Solution of the Body; and in order to this, he muft take it in a convenient place, and propofe to himfelf the right way, that he be not feduced into devious Paths. Secondly he muft obferve the Governance of the Fire, taking Care that it be neither too much, nor too little, or too hot, or too cold. For the fumm of all is fited in an exact Governance of the Fire; by which the vivifying *Spirits* of *Antimony* are extracted, and loofed from their bonds, and fo rendered capable to manifeft their Effects operatively. Alfo he muft take great Care, that this Operative Vertue be not mortifyed and perifh by Aduftion. Thirdly, the Ufe or Dofe is to be obferved by him, that he may adminifter it in due manner, knowing the Meafure, as I above mentioned, when I fpake of the five principal Heads requifite in the Exercife and Practice of *Chymiftry*; but here I only hint at it curforily by way of a Parable.

By *Refolution* the fum of the Matter is propofed, but by Fire it is prepared to profit. For a Butcher cuts out an Ox, and divides it into parts, but no Man can profitably enjoy this Flefh, unlefs he firft boyl it by Fire, by which Operation the Red Subftance of the Flefh is changed and prepared into white Aliment. If a Man conftrained by hunger, fhould eat that Raw and Red Flefh, it would be Venom to him rather than *Medicine*;

becaufe

becaufe the natural Heat of the Stomach is too weak to concoct and digeft that crude Body. Hence, my dear Friend, you may conclude, that fince *Antimony* hath greater Venom, and a more grofs Mineral Body than Animal Flefh (as by the above recited common Example I have already fhewed) it will alfo prove more perillous, if ufed Crude, without Preparation, Separation and Coction by Fire; yea it will be and remain Venom, which will fuddenly kill the Sick. Therefore the Venenofity of *Antimony* is fo to be taken away, as it may never again be converted into Venom, after the fame manner, as Wine, which being once, by putrefaction and corruption turned into Vinegar, never afterward yeilds any Spirit of Wine, but always is and remains Vinegar. But on the Contrary, if the Spirit only of the Wine be feparated, and the Aquofity left by it felf, and the fame Spirit afterward exalted, it will never in any wife be changed into Vinegar, although it fhould be kept an hundred Years; but will always remain Spirit of Wine, no otherwife, then as Vinegar remains Vinegar.

This Tranfmutation of Wine into Vinegar is a wonderful Thing; becaufe fomewhat is produced from Wine, which was not before in its vegetable Effence. In which it is alfo to be noted, that in diftillation of Wine the Spirit firft comes forth; but (on the contrary) in diftilling Vinegar the Phlegm firft comes, afterward the Spirit, as I have fhewed above in its own place, where I alfo made mention of this Example. Therefore Spirit of Wine makes Bodies volatile, becaufe it felf is volatile; but Spirit of Vinegar fixeth all Medicaments, as well of Minerals as Vegetables, and renders them folid; fo that they apprehend things fixed, and expel fixed Difeafes.

* Confider

* Confider and obferve thefe things diligently; for this principal Key is of great concern.
Therefore *Antimony*, which contains in it felf its
own Vinegar, ought to be fo prepared, as all its
Venenofity may be taken away, and he, who ufeth
it, conceives no Venom thereby, but rather drives
away and cafts out all Poyfon from himfelf, by
the ufe thereof.

> * *Believe not only* Bafilius, *but me alfo, with the fame Faith and fin-*
> *cerity affirming to you; This is the firft Key, this is the principal part of*
> *the whole Art, this opens to you the firft Gate, this will alfo unlock the laft,*
> *which leads to the Palace of the King. But as I faid, not only believe,*
> *but alfo confider and obferve. Here you ftand in the Entrance, if you mifs*
> *the Door, all your Courfe will be Error, all your Haft Ruine, and all your Wif-*
> *dom Foolifhnefs. He who obtains this Key, and knows the Method (which*
> *is called Manual Operation) by which to ufe it, and hath ftrength to turn the*
> *fame, will acquire Riches, aud an open Paffage unto the Myfteries of Chy-*
> *miftry.*

Therefore Preparation of Antimony confifts in
the Key of Alchimy, by which it is diffolved, o-
pened, divided and feparated; as in *Calcination*,
Reverberation, *Sublimation*, &c. as we declared
above of it. Alfo in extracting its Effence, and in
vivifying its Mercury; which Mercury muft afterward bee precipited into a fixed Pouder. Likewife by Art and a due Method, of it may be made
an Oyl, which is effectual wholly to confume that
new and unknown Difeafe, which the *French*, in
their Warlike Expeditions, brought into our Re-
gions. The fame is vifible in other Preparations,
derived from the *Spagyrick* Art and Alchimy; as for
Example: If any one would make Beer of Barley,
Wheat, or other Corn, all thefe degrees muft
be moft perfectly known to him, before he
can from thofe Grains extract their moft fubtil
Effence and virtue, and reduce the fame into a moft
efficacious Drink. Firft, the Grains muft be fo
long

long steeped in Water, as untill they be able sufficiently, to open and resolve themselves (as I, when
I was a Young Man, travelling into *England* and
Holland, diligently observed to be done in those
places) this is called *Putrefaction* and *Corruption*.
This Key being used, the Water is drawn off
from the Grain, and the macerated Corn is laid on
Heaps close together, and left so for a due time,
until it spontaneously conceive heat, and by the
same heat germinating, the Grains adhere each to
other: this is *Digestion*. This being finished, the
Grains which adhered in their Germination, are
separated, and dryed, either in the Air, or by Heat
of Fire, and so hardned. This is *Reverberation*, and
Coagulation. When the Corn is thus prepared, it is
carried to the Mill, that it may be broak and
ground small; this is *Vegetable Calcination*. Afterward, by Heat of Fire cocting these Grains, the
more noble Spirit of them is extracted, and the
Water is imbibed with the same; which without
the aforesaid Preparation could not have been.
This way the crude Water is converted into Beer,
and this Operation (though I speak but rudely)
is and is called *Distillation*. The *Hops*, when added to the Beer, is the *Vegetable* Salt thereof,
which conserves and preserves from all Contraries,
endeavouring to corrupt the same. This way of
boyling Water into Drink, by extraction of the
Spirits from the Grains, the *Spaniards* and *Italians*
know not, and in my native Soyl of *Germany*
about the *Rhine*, few are found skilled in this
Art.

After all these works are performed, a new
Separation is made by *Clarification*, viz. of the Drink,
in this manner: a little *Yest* or *Ferment* is added,
which excites an internal Motion and Heat in the
Beer, so that it is elevated in it self, and (by the
help

help of time) *Separation* of the dense from the rare, and of the pure from the impure is made; and by this means the Beer acquires a constant virtue in Operating, so that it penetrates and effects all those *Ends*, for which it was made and brought into use : which before could not have been; because the Spirit, the Operator was hindred, by its own Impurity, from effecting its proper Work.

In Wine also doth not Experience teach the same? that cannot, before the time come, in which the impuritys may be separated from it, so very perfectly and efficaciously perform its own Work*, as after Separation of the pure from the impure : which by Drunkeness is manifest; for Beer or Wine unsettled, and not purifyed, give not forth from themselves so much Spirit for inebriating, as after Clarification. But of this no more. After all the aforesaid, a new Operation may be instituted, by Vegetable sublimation, for separation of the Spirit of the Wine or Beer, and for preparing it by Distillation into another Drink of *Burning Wine*, which may also be made of the Lees or Dregs of Wine and Beer. When this is done, the Operative Virtue is separated from its own Body, and the Spirit being extracted by Fire, forsakes its own unprofitable dead Habitation, in which it was commodiously hospited before. Now, if this *Burning Wine*, or Spirit of Wine, be rectifyed, an Exaltation is made by often distilling it, and by a certain method of Operating, the pure part (free from all Phlegm or Aquosity) may be so concentred, and as it were condensed, as one Measure of it may effect more, then twenty or more could have done before. For it sooner inebriates, and is swift, volatile and subtil for penetrating and operating.

* Here I admonish you, whosoever you are, who

who defire to be taught by my Writings , and hope to obtain Riches and a true Medicine from *Antimony* , that you would not careleſly peruſe my Intention , in which is no letter writ in vain , and which hath not a certain ſingular ſignification for your Inſtruction.

Come hither you Traveller, ſtay your Journy here. Contemn not or ſlightly paſs over this tautological , but not impertinent , Admonition ; often in your mind have recourſe to this Deſcription of Beer , ſearch , contemplate , and weigh all Things , perhaps in this turbid and famous Gulf , you will find the Fiſh you look not for. If in this Light you yet be blind , I know not any Collyrium will profit you : if with ſo certain a manuduction you cannot paſs on to the work it ſelf , I know not who will lend you a Staff, or what Demonſtration can direct the Journy of a ſtupid Man. Beleive , read , meditate , labour , and ſpare the uſe of ſo many Chymical Books , which diſtract you with the Error of various ways , this one tells you all Things.

Yea, I here ſolemnly affirm, that there are many words diſperſed here and there in my Writings, to which if the Reader give heed as he ought, and know in what Fundamentals the principal Heads of the matter are ſited , and as it were buryed , he will have no Cauſe to repent his often turning over the ſame Leaves , but will eſteem every word as much, as a peice of Gold Coyn. For you know, that although the Examples by me propoſed , ſound harſh , as delivered in a rude manner , yet they contain in them ſomewhat that is excellent and of great Moment. Yet I am not here ambitious to procure Authority or praiſe to my Writings , which is not my Buſineſs , nor would it become me : for when the Operation of them ſhall be brought to Light , they will acquire praiſe enough to themſelves. I purpoſely and willingly produce Examples ſo rude and common , becauſe the power of *Antimony* and the true Virtue thereof, deeply and profoundly abſconded in its inmoſt parts , is to be ſearched out. I was willing,

ling, by theſe groſs Examples to lead you by the
hand, and ſhew you the way, that by them you
might attain to the Thing it ſelf, and not at the
very firſt err from the Gate ; for ſo doing you
would long wander, and never bring your Operation to the deſired End. For *Antimony* is like a
Bird, which is carryed through the *Air* and as
the Wind drives it, ſo it turns it ſelf which
way that wills : here, in this Caſe, Man acts the
Part of the *Air* or Wind, and can drive and move
Antimony, at his pleaſure, and repoſe it in ſuch a
place, as himſelf chooſeth : he can imbibe it,
with a yellow, red, white, or black Colour, according as he deſires it ſhould be, and as he rules
and governs the Fire; becauſe in *Antimony* (as
in *Mercury*) all Colours are found ; which no Man
ſhould wonder at, conſidering how many Things
Nature bears abſconded in her Boſom, which
neither you nor I are able to comprehend in many
days.

    If a Book happen to be given to a Man, that
is unlearned, he knows not what is ſignifyed by
that Writing, or what that Scripture intends; for it
is hid from his Eyes, and he ſtands amazed, as a Cow
at the ſight of a new Door. But if unto that unlearned Man, any one ſuggeſt the Explication of
the Book, and teach him not only the matter
contained therein, but alſo the uſe of the ſame, the
Man no more admires it, as an Art; but by this
means it becomes to him a Common Thing, the
Reaſon and Operation of which he underſtands,
and by his own Study he can learn, conceive, and
comprehend the Utility ſo perfectly, as now
none of thoſe Things, which were contained in
the Book, are hid from him; becauſe he hath
learned both to read and underſtand what is written therein. Such a Book is *Antimony* to thoſe,

who

who know not the Art of Reading ; therefore
I faithfully admonifh all, who defire to be partakers of its Utilities, to bend their mind to
know and pronounce the letters thereof, that
fo they may acquire the Art of Reading that
Book ; and in fuch a manner, that (as in a
School) they may be removed from Form to
Form; when he who hath rightly gained Experience, fhall prefide as *Rector*, and judge of that,
which in Trial is moft worthy : for One is worthy
to be preferred before another, in the Poffeffion
of that.

But here, what comes into my mind, and
ought in no wife to be paffed over in Silence, I
think good to mention ; *viz :* that at this Day
many are found who exclaim, and rafhly pronounce *Crucifige*, *Crucifige*, againft all thofe, who
prepare Venoms into Medicaments, by which (as
they fay) many Mortals perifh, or, if they efcape
with Life, live miferably; fuch are *Mercury*, *Arfe-
nick*, *Antimony*, *&c.* and this Clamour is cheifly
made by thofe, who (if it pleafe the *GODS*) are
called *Doctors* * of Medicine, yet indeed underftand not what the difference is, between Venom,
and Medicine, but are wholly ignorant how Venom may be prepared, fo as to pafs into a falutary Medicament; and inftead of its malignity, put
on a better Nature.

---

* Bafilius *fomewhat indulgeth his own* Genius, *inveighing againft*
Falfe-Phyfitians, *whofe ignorance (in his time) was fo very great, as they
contemned every fublime Preparation of Medicine, which he himfelf, and
Chymifts with him did profefs; prefcribing the fame as unprofitable, perillous,
and hurtful : againft whom, it is not ftrange, if the* Chymifts (*on the other
hand) rofe up with fome fmall vehemency, and endeavour couragioufly, by
affiftance of their Knowledge and Confcience, to break through that Rout of
unskilful Men ; but the beft Things are not allways the moft profperous.* Chymifts *overcame by the Juftice of their Caufe, but were overcome by Number :
yet, having verity and goodnefs on their fide, they fought with fo great*

Confidence, as they were certainly assured they should bear away the Victory; *which our* Author *here shews, and* Paracelsus *(prophesying of the Coming of* Elias *the* Artist *) did presage would be. And certainly unto me (seriously considering how greatly* Chymists *have in these times improved their Knowledge) the* Dawning *of that Day hath opened it self, since I behold so many Rays of the approaching* Sun.

Against these I do in a special manner exclaim and protest, against these, I say, who (ignorant of *Preparation*) exhibit *Poyson* to Men: for *Mercury, Auripigment, Antimony*, and such like, are venoms in their Subftance, and unless rightly prepared remain Venoms. Yet after a Legitimate Preparation, all their Venenosity is broke, extinguished and expelled, so that no part of them remains, but what is *Medicine*, which refists all internal Venoms, although most deeply rooted, and radically destroys the same. For *Venom*, being in such a manner prepared, as it can no longer hurt, refists all *Poyson*, which is not as yet prepared, and so very well prepares and subjugates it, as it is compelled with the same to put off its own venomous Nature.

Here I shall raise a great Contention among the Learned; for I know they will doubt what these my Words should signify, as whether what I affirm and write be possible to be done or no; and they will be divided into several Opinions thereabout. Some will judge it is in no wise possible, that from those Things, of which we treat, the venenosity should be wholly taken away; nor do I wonder, that they persift in that Opinion, since the Doctrine of like Preparations is absolutely unknown to them, who have not the least thought of that, which leads to the Knowledge of these more profound Mysteries. Yet a small part of these Men will with me be constrained to acknowledge, it is possible a vile Thing may be changed into

into a better. For you (you *Doctors* I mean) muſt
confeſs to me, that your purpoſe is to reduce
that Evil, from which the Diſeaſe had its Original, into a better State. Go to then; will you not
alſo grant, that if any Evil be in thoſe Things, of
which *Medicine* is to be made, the ſame Evil muſt
be converted into a better State, that it may ſo
much the better perform its operation, and more
powerfully and profitably act, without any notable peril? But ſince unto very few as yet is known,
or by Experience found, the Way, by which a
Man ought to proceed in theſe Preparations, a
very ſmall part of theſe will aſſume and contend
for the Opinion I here affirm, and publickly profeſs : for very many will be carryed away with
the greater Rout, crying, *Venom*, *Venom*! which
Voyces, whilſt I hear them, put me in mind
of thoſe wild Clamours, by which the *Jews* required the *Saviour* and *Redeemer* of the World,
that he might ſuffer the Puniſhment of the *Croſs*,
often crying out *Crucify him*, *Crucify him*, whom
they proclaimed to be the higheſt, moſt preſent,
moſt pernitious, and curſed *Venom*, when as indeed he was the nobleſt, ſupreme, moſt glorious
and moſt profitable *Medicine* of our *Souls*, which
was to deliver us from the Death of *Sinners*, from
the *Devil*, *Hell* and all *Misfortunes*. Although
thoſe proud *Phariſees* and Lawyers neither could
nor would underſtand this, neverthelefs he both
then was, and will be to the end of the *World*, and
after it to all *Eternity*, the ſame ſuperexcellent *Medicine* : and neither the *Devil*, nor Death, nor the
very Gates of *Hell*, nor any *Creature*, how powerful, or perverſe ſoever, can effect any thing at
all, whereby to overthrow this Truth.

So I hope, yea doubt not (although all vagabond and circumforaneous *Medicaſters*, all *Phyſitians*

tians reſident in *Cities*, and how many ſoever there
be, that profeſs themſelves *Maſters* of any part
of *Medicine*; do all together contrive what they
can, and exclaim againſt *Antimony*) but that the
ſame *Antimony* will triumph over the ingratitudes
of all thoſe unskilful Men (for true *Phyſitians* and
ſuch as are always ready to learn, I touch not
here) and by its own power and virtue acquired
after due preparation, will overcome and tread under foot all its Enemies. But, on the contrary,
thoſe ignorant falſe Judges, and pertinacious contemners of *Antimony*, becauſe they know not the
Truth, together with the proud and blood-thirſty
Jews, ſhall periſh, and be caſt into the Abyſs of
Hell. How ridiculous thoſe magnificent, and to
themſelves only wiſe *Doctors*, ſeem to me, who
deterr *Emperors*, *Kings*, *Princes*, and all other
Great Men, and ſeriouſly admoniſh them not ſo
much as to touch ſuch *Medicines* with their Lips, becauſe they are noxious, venomous, and every way
perillous, I will not here declare, ſince I ſee them
only to judge according to their own Opinion,
without entertaining any Obſervations of other
things, the Knowledge of which they have not
before acquired by their own Contemplation,
and therefore cannot judge of any thing elſe, or
otherwiſe than they have learned. Therefore to
theſe I ſay, if there be any Man, that hath taken ſo
ſtrong a *Poyſon*, as preſent Death is neceſſarily expected to follow, I will (provided the Man be
left wholly to my Care) give him an *Antidote* by
me prepared which ſhall continually reſiſt that
Venom, and quickly expel it out of the Body. But
I little care, whether you Mr. *Doctor*, who do
neither know this Thing, nor ever would apply
your mind to know it, do ſlight the ſame, and
repute it as a ridiculous, and altogether falſe tale;

it is

it is fufficient for me, that I am able (but if praife
worthy, let praife be given to *G O D)* to prove
and defend the Truth thereof. For I my felf
have experienced it, I have made, I have prepared,
I have prefcribed this Medicine, and there wants
not a fufficient number of Witneffes to confirm it
under Hand and Seal.

And whenfoever I fhall have occafion to contend in the School with fuch a Doctor, who knows
not how himfelf to prepare his own Medicines,
but commits that Bufinefs to another, I am fure I
fhall obtain the Palm from her: for indeed that
good Man knows not what Medicines he pre-
fcribes to the Sick; whether the Colour of them
be white, black, grey or blew, he cannot tell; nor
doth this wretched man know, whether the Medicament he gives be dry or hot, cold or humid; but
he only knows, that he found it fo written in his
Books, and thence pretends Poffeffion (or as it were
Poffeffion) by Prefcription of a very long time:
yet he defires no further Information. Here again
let it be lawful to exclaim, good *G O D;* to what
a ftate is the matter brought! what goodnefs of
mind is in thefe men! what care do they take of
the Sick! Wo, wo to them! in the day of Judgment they will find the fruit of their ignorance
and rafhnefs; then they will fee him whom they
pierced, when they neglected their Neighbour;
fought after Money and nothing elfe: whereas
were they cordial in their Profeffion; they would
fpend Nights and Days in Labour, that they might
become more learned in their Art, whence more
certain health would accrew to the Sick with their
Eftimation, and greater glory to themfelves. But
fince Labour is tedious to them, they commit the
matter to Chance, and being fecure of their Honour and content with their Fame, they (like Braw-

lers) defend themfelves with a certain Garrulity, without any refpect had to Confcience or Truth; Coals feem wonderful ftrange, and as out-landifh Wares to them, therefore they fpare the Money, that fhould be beftowed in them, as if they intended to lay it out to a better ufe. *Vulcan* himfelf, *viz.* the Prepairer of Medicaments, is not found among them; for their Fornaces ftand in the Apothecaries Shop, to which they feldom or never come. A Paper Scrol in which their ufual *Recipe* is written, ferves their purpofe to the full, which Bill being by fome Apothecaries Boy or Servant received, he with great noyfe thumps out of his Mortar every Medicine, and all the Health of the Sick.

My *GOD*, change, change thefe times, and and put an end to this arrogant Pride, overturn thofe Trees, left they fwell up to Heaven, throw down thofe Giants left they accumulate all Mountains; and defend thofe, who ferioufly managing their Bufinefs, faithfully ferve thee, that they may be able to ftand againft thefe their Perfecutors. I ferioufly admonifh all thofe in our Monaftery, bound by the fame Vows with me, that they would with my felf Night and Day pray unto *GOD*, that he would fo illuminate thefe Enemies of true Medicine, as they may execrate their own Error, and acknowledge the Glory of *GOD*, and his Power infited in the Creatures, and perceive the Clearnefs latent in them, by Preparation and Anatomy (as it were fpeaking in their Ears) which otherwife furrounded and covered over with external Impurities, would deeply be concealed, and never brought to Light. But I truft the *Creator* of all Things, (both of thofe which fall under our Senfe, and of thofe that are remote from our Senfes) will benignly hear our Prayers; that, if not whilft I

and

and my Brethren live, yet after our Death, such a Conversion of Things and Men (*G O D* answer these Desires) may follow, as that thick and obscure Veil may be taken away from the Eyes of our Enemies, and they by true and infallible Illumination, obtain a clear light, that they may find their lost Groat: which *G O D* the eternal Governour of Times and Things of his Grace and Mercy grant.

But it is fit, that I, who intended to publish a certain Discourse of Antimony, in all its Numbers absolute, should begin with the * Name it self.

* *Poets do often posit in the midst of their Poems, Histories or Fables of Princes, that by a continued Series of Things, they may the more easily attain their End, which is to delight their Readers:* Chymists *for another end use the same* Medium. *For since their purpose is to teach the Readers so, as they may only be understood by those, who wholly devote themselves with a fervent desire to the Study of that Science, they keep not that Order, which proceeds from the beginning to the End by Mediums. Therefore our Author, at length coming to treat of the Name of* Antimony, *whence it took beginning, acts as another Man addicted to some Scholastick Order: but by and by turning from this Discourse, he answers an Objection, before it is made by Interrogation; viz. whether from* Antimony *all its Venome may be taken away, the possibility of which he proves by very profitable and significant Examples.*

The *Arabians*, to whom in times past this Mineral was known, did in their Language call it *Asinat*; but the *Chaldeans* called it *Stibium*; among the *Latines* at this day the Name of *Antimony* is used, by which name they first of all signified it. We *Germans* in our Language have given it a Name, which seems to express a certain property of its Nature; for since it is seen to consist of a certain streiked Matter, and of it may easily be made Glass endued with various Colours, which proceed there from, we have called it *Spies-glass*, as if we should say streiked Glass. From which Variety of the Name, by a prudent Judgment, a

D 2   singular

fingular Colleftion may be made, *viz.* that *Antimony* was known, and greatly efteemed, and its virtue and Utility obferved and brought into ufe by the *Arabians*, *Chaldeans*, *Latins*, and our *Germans :* but afterward, the Herefies of various Opinions arifing, the ufe was vitiated, and its Virtue and Glory firft obfcured, and afterward wholly extinguifhed. Of which there is no Reafon to Doubt; for nothing is more probable, than that Truth fhould fuffer Dammage and Shipwrack by the Oppreffion of Enemies. For who knows not the Malice of the Devil, which by Reafon of our Sins and Blindnefs is very often permitted by *GOD.* The Devil is the perpetual Enemy of Mankind, who imploys all his Strength, and all his Deceits, and omits nothing, which in himfelf is, to prevent the Knowledge of the profit of true Medecine, and to exterminate its ufe ; knowing well enough, that by that means the power and glory of *GOD* is obfcured, and thofe Sacrifices of the praifes of men are impeded, by which they gave thanks to *GOD*, becaufe he hath infited as it were the Rayes of his Goodnefs in the Creatures, whence they may obtain Health by a natural auxiliary.

But fince to difcourfe of the Name of *Antimony*, is not to our purpofe, we will defift from this Matter. For all the Praife of *Antimony* confifts in the Preparation thereof, which is made for perfecting the Virtues infufed in it from Nature by the *Author* of *Nature.* Therefore my difcourfe fhall be of this, handling it and its known Virtue, and I will endeavour to make my Name immortal. Yet before I come to declare the Virtue of *Antimony*, fince I above confeffed, that it is meer Venom, I would have you know and diligently note, that Venom is able to draw Venom to it felf, becaufe like it felf, much fooner and much more than any other Thing of another Nature.   Now

Now let any Reader confider, and obferve it as
a Thing worthy of Note, that the true *Unicorns-*
horn, fophifticated by no fallacy, repels all Venom
from it felf, nor can it affume or draw to it felf a-
ny thing of Venom, as is manifeft by Experience.
Let a living Spider be put in a Circle made of *Uni-*
corns-horn, and out of this Circle it cannot go, or
pafs over the *Unicorns-horn*, for it fhuns whatfoever is adverfe to Venom. But if the Circle be
made of venemous Matter, it is not to be doubted,
but that the Spider will go out of it, and pafs over
that Venom like it felf. Note this Experiment,
make a piece of Silver hollow, and put it in Water,
that it may float like a Boat, and put Venom to it,
then hold a piece of true Unicorns-Horn, as nigh
to it as you can, but fo as you may not touch it,
that Unicorns-Horn by its fpiritual Virtue will
drive the Silver from it, fo that it will flie away
like a Duck, which fwimming on the Water flies,
when it perceives the Snares of the Fowler ready
to entangle it. But on the contrary, Nature in a
wonderful manner loves and follows its own like,
as appears by this Example. Put a little piece of
pure and fine Bread in a difh full of Water, fo as the
Bread may fwim upon the Water, hold a piece of
true Unicorns-Horn clofe to it, yet fo as it touch it
not; and if you leifurely move the Unicorns-Horn
the little piece of Bread will follow it. Nature
fo much loves its own like, and fo much hates what
is unlike it felf, as this flies, and that follows.
Therefore let our *Doctors* confider, that Venom by
a certain Magnetick Power Attracts Venom, and
thofe things which are void of Venom, do in like
manner draw to themfelves things pure, and wanting a Venomous quality.

Therefore Venom may be taken away two ways;
firft, by its Contrary, which refifts Venom, as already

ready is related of the Unicorns-Horn. Secondly, by Like, when Venom by a certain Magnetick
power draws Venom to it ſelf. But the Venom
which muſt heal Venom like it ſelf, ought firſt to
be ſo prepared, as its Venom may paſs into Medicine, and by its own attractive virtue, aſſume the
other to and expel it with it ſelf. Of which thing
you have a moſt clear Example in *Soap:* That is
compounded of Oyl and other fat ingredient Matters, which ſeem to be, and in very deed are, more
apt to foul, than cleanſe Linen; but becauſe in the
Boyling of the Soap, eſpecially by the help of Salt,
a certain Separation and Preparation is made, the
Soap is rendred moſt apt to draw to it ſelf and waſh
out all foulneſs and filths from Linen and other
things: ſo indeed may Venom in a certain manner,
by Antecedent Preparation be accommodated ſo, as
to be no more Venom, but a Medicament, it draws
to it ſelf all other Poyſon, caſts it out, and reſtores
the man to his priſtine Purity and Health.

Now ſince our Diſcourſe hath led us ſo far, and
we have begun to open Nature ſo much; that the
truly Studious of Medicine (though hitherto ignorant of this) may clearly know, what Good or E-
vil is latent in Nature, what is Venom and what
is harmleſs; which is a thing hath not as yet been
found out by Doctors, by reaſon of their own ſupine
negligence; and that the Truth thereof may be
demonſtrated and alſo confirmed, it will not be a-
miſs to produce certain Experimental Examples,
which may diſcover the Truth, and refute the falſe
Opinions of others. Put an Egg, which in the
Winter is congealed with Cold, into very cold
Water, there let it lie for a due ſpace of time, and
the Ice will externally adhere to the Egg-ſhell, but
the Cold be extracted from the Egg it ſelf, and reſtored to its priſtine vigour and intireneſs. Again,

if

if any Member be benummed with Cold, let not the Patient neglect himself, but apply cold Snow-water round about, so one Cold attracts the other, and the Member is restored. On the contrary, if any One have a Member inflamed, let him apply to that Inflammation an hot Matter ; as for Example, Spirit of Wine, which is mere Fire, or the Quintessence of Sulphur, and he will in very deed find, that Heat is attracted by Heat, in a certain Magnetick manner, and like to rejoyce in like, and not only to asswage the pain and heat of the inflamed Member, but absolutely to restore the same to its pristine strength.

Yet left this our purpose should not be fully enough confirmed by Examples, I will also add another, by way of Supplement. Take Frog-Spawn in the Moneth of *March*, and laying it on a Board dry it in the Sun, when dry reduce it to Powder, and strew of this Powder, upon Wounds made by Venomous Vipers or Serpents ; by this means such Wounds will be so prepared, as they may be perfectly healed by other Medicaments applied thereunto. Or otherwise, if Linen cloaths be often moistned in Frog-Spawn, and as often dried, and that Linen cut into small pieces and applied to Wounds, they effect the same, as the aforesaid Powder would have done. But that the very foundation of this Truth may more clearly be declared ; take a venomous Toad, dry him in the Sun, shut him up in an Earthen closed Pot, and by burning reduce him to Ashes ; then having taken out the Ashes, and reduced the same to Powder, apply of that Powder to a Wound made by Venom, and this Poyson attracts the other Poyson, and joyns it with it self. Why so, I pray ? Because by this Burning, which is the Calcination of the Toad, its interior Virtue is made manifest, and efficacious for opera-

ting ;

tiug; fo, that Like can attract like, and efpecially
Venom Venom, to it felf. Therefore firmly perfwade your felf, that this Truth is infallible and
immutable, which I have here propofed to you and
others by Example. If any One afflicted with the
Peft, do diligently obferve this, he will find the
Truth of thofe Things I have here above mentioned : the *Aftrum* of *Sol*, and the Spirit of *Mercury*,
miniftred in a Peftilential Seafon, preferve many.
For the Spirit of *Mercury* doth alfo draw to it felf
its own like, and hath in it felf the Medicament,
and attractive power of all venomous Difeafes.
Yet fince the *Aftrum* of *Sol*, from which (as from
an operative and all vivifying Sun) all things in
their kinds univerfally arife; therefore I determine that in the potency of Gold, more than in
all other Things, is an Operating Nature; that is,
in its own *Aftrum*, whence both it felf, and all Metals and Minerals, in the Beginning, received
their firft Nativity and Propagation of Generation. Touching which more may be faid, when I
fhall manifeft to you the *Aftrum* of *Sol*, and commend the fame moft religioufly to your Confcience.

After the fame manner procefs is to be made with
Antimony, which hath the fame Operations with
corporal Gold; yet of the *Aftrum* thereof I now
fpeak not. For I know (faith *Antimony*) it be-
hoves me, before that, to fear and tremble; although in many principal *Arcanums* of Medicine,
I far excel it; yet univerfally I am able to effect
none of thofe Things, which the *Aftrum* of *Sol*
(confirmed by the Teftimony of Celeftial Verity)
is able to produce. The *Aftrum* of *Mercury* I
omit, becaufe I my felf have my defcent from the
fame Original with it: but as to a Celeftial penetrating power of Operating, I give the firft place
of

of Dominion to the *Aſtrum* of *Sol.*

My Writings and Books, compoſed by Experience, properly follow and anſwer each to other;
as one Metal (as to its virtue) is obſerved and e-
ſteemed by another, and muſt by Fire be proved of
what value it is. So theſe my Sayings, or Writings,
or Medicaments, ought to be brought into the
Schools, as tending to one Scope and End. Into
the Schools, I ſay, where Riches obtain to themſelves (as it were) an Hereditary place, and inſtead
of that take away all the Honour, which is due to
Vulcan only, who can boaſt himſelf to be a Maſter
in his own Element of Fire. Which may be ſhewed by Example, and a true and manifeſt *Proof.*
When moſt hard Steel is ſtruck with an hard and
ſolid Flint, Fire excites Fire by vehement Commotion, and accenſion, drawing forth the occult Sulphur, or the occult Fire is manifeſted by that vehement Commotion, and enkindled by the Air ſo,
as it truly and efficaciouſly burns; but the *Salt*
remains in the Aſhes, and the *Mercury* thence takes
its flight together with the burning Sulphur.*

* *You, who read this moſt ſimple Compariſon of Steel and a Flint, ſlack the*
Reins of your Admiration, and ſeriouſly ask your ſelf, whether there can be
found out any way or Method, by which from this Stone and Cold Iron may be
extracted, a Subſtance, of which one only Grain (but why do I ſpeak of a
Grain?) of which the hundred part of a Grain can in a very ſhort time
Convert a great Maſs of ſome rude Matter, into the moſt ſplendid and moſt pre-
tious of all Things; yea, into Fire moſt profitable for Mankind? This is
poſſible, and is dayly done, when the fixed is made Volatile, and the Volatile
again fixed. He that hath underſtanding, let him underſtand, and ceaſe to
defame the admirable virtues of Chymical Works.

So here alſo underſtand, that *Antimony* ought in
a certain Method ſo to be handled, as its *Mercury*
may be ſeparated from the Sulphur thereof, in a
Natural Manner. Now, as Fire, which lies abſconded in Matter, unleſs it be made manifeſt, and

can

can be demonſtrated, is profitable for nothing, is not (as I may ſay) tangible by the Hands, nor can it effect any thing to purpoſe; ſo Medicine can effect nothing that is excellent, unleſs it be firſt ſeparated from its Grofsneſs, rectified and ſo diſcharged of Impurities, clarified and brought to Light by due Preparation, as is manifeſt in all Things: for when Separation of the pure from the impure is made, and all that is mountanous or terreſtrial is ſegregated from the pure Metal, then the deſired Harveſt is to be expected. Hence it is manifeſt, that Fire can effect nothing, before it is in a certain manner opened and ſet at Liberty, that it may operate. Therefore, to comprehend much in few Words, I ſay, this is the Condition of *Antimony*. Whatſoever is occult and abſconded from the Knowledge of the Vulgar, that injoys the Name and Honour of Art, *viz.* as long as it lies hid; but ſo ſoon as it is diſcovered and made manifeſt, Art hath end, and it becomes a Mechanick Work; as I have more than once declared in other of my Books.

A Bee ſucks Honey from Flowers, with ſuch Art as the Almighty hath inſited in it, in which Honey is latent a Virtue, Juice, and Corroborative Power, of which a Medicine is made, as is obvious to the Eyes of all Men. Now, from that *Honey*, of a ſweet and moſt pleaſant Taſte, a violent Corroſive and preſent Venom may be prepared; which perhaps no man, unleſs he who hath learned it, will believe; no man certainly conſiders this, unleſs he be a diligent Obſerver. Yet for this Cauſe Honey is not to be contemned, nor is it to be ſaid, that although it hath a moſt grateful Sweetneſs, yet it is a Corrupt Medicine; becauſe a Corroſive may be made of it: but it ſhould rather be ſaid, that Corruption proceeds from the Phyſicians ignorance,

rance, who knew not how duely to prepare it.
Here I am willing to teach the ignorant Phyſician,
to free him from the laſt Judgment. For Honey
is prepared of the Superfluities of Brute Animals,
by which the Grounds and Fields are fatned; in
thoſe Grounds ariſe Flowers, Herbs, Fruit-Trees
of various kinds, from which the Bees ſuck a moſt
noble Quinteſſence : by this is made the Alteration
and Generation of one Thing into another, *viz.*
into Aliment of another Form and Taſte, which
in no wiſe agrees with the former, and that is called Honey. Of ſuch Honey is prepared a Food
moſt grateful, pleaſant and fit for man, and for
many Things moſt profitable. Of the ſame may
be prepared a Poyſon moſt hurtful to Man and
Beaſt.

Therefore, do you Searcher of Nature, of what
Age, Sex, Fortune or Condition ſoever, follow me
and Nature. I will ſhew you the Truth, without
any Mixture of falſity, drawn from the very Foundation. I will make you underſtand, who proceeds rightly, and who unadviſedly. I will teach
you to ſeparate the Good from the Evil, the Higheſt from the Loweſt. For of *Antimony*, if its Venom be firſt changed into Remedy, is made a Medicine, which eradicates, and like Fire penetrates,
prepares and by coƈting conſumes all Diſeaſes.
Wherefore *Antimony* is firſt to be prepared into a
true *Stone*, which is the Quinteſſence thereof; and
becauſe, in its Operation it is altogether like unto
Fire, (when reduced to its Coagulation) it ſhall by
me be named the *Stone* of *Fire*. When this *Stone*
of *Fire* is rightly prepared, as in the End of this
Treatiſe I will further ſhew, its Medicinal Virtue
conſumes all noxious Humours, purifies the Blood
in the higheſt Degree, and performs all that may
be effeƈted by *Aurum potabile.*

Therefore,

Therefore, I pray you, my unexperienced Doctor, who have neither learned my Preparation, nor
conceived the Uſe, not to judge from a falſe Suſpi-
tion, and your own ignorant Thoughts ; but ſet
about the Work it ſelf, and learn how the Preparation of *Antimony* ought to be made, how you ſhould
further proceed with it, how its Venom is expelled
and ſeparated, and Salutary Medicine poſited in the
place of it, and exalted.   When I ſay * you ſhall
have performed This, then at length will you be
able to judge of the difference, and underſtand
thoſe things, which before were very far remote
from your Knowledge.

* *Here again the* Author *waxeth hot againſt falſe Phyſicians ; but do you
read on, and after this Heat be will give you a proſitable Doctrine, which you
may ſoon find in* Aqua Fortis *and* Spirit *of* Wine.

O you wretched and to be pitied *Medicaſters*,
who painted with a *Fucus*, breath out I know not
what *Thraſonick* Brags, and paſs over Mountains
wanting Foundation, walking through Clouds in
your own Thoughts, and know not where at length
you ſhall reſt your Foot: you, I ſay, I admoniſh to
conſider what you will anſwer, in the Extream Judgment of the Son of GOD.   *Seek,* and when you
have found, convert what you find to uſe, and ſo
performing your Office commit the Reſt to GOD,
who will give ſucceſs, and never leave you deſtitute
of help.   But you infamous men, more mad than
Bacchanalian Fools, who will neither learn, nor ſoul
your Hands with Coals, judge not left you procure
Judgment to be pronounced againſt you, which
your Childrens Children may write down to your
ſhame in an undeleble Character.
Every Phyſician ought above all Things to take
Care, that he do neither leſs nor more, than procure

cure the Reſtitution of Health loſt, not inſtituting
his Curation contrary to Nature, or deviating from
her direct Intention. When Spirit of Wine is
poured upon *Aqua Fortis* a vehement Ebullition is
made, and theſe two Natures will not eaſily permit themſelves to be together ; but he, that knows
how by Diſtillation to conjoyn and unite them, according to the true Intention of Philoſophers, he
may uſe them in many things for good. After
the ſame manner , Oyl or Liquor of Tartar, and
Vinegar made of Rich Wine, act each upon other ;
for they hate and fly from each other, as Fire and
Water, although they proceeded from one and the
ſame Matter. Therefore the Phyſician ought in
a ſpecial manner to be mindful, to underſtand all
Circumſtances from the Sick very exactly, and conſider the ſame being underſtood that in Curing he
may uſe ſuch Means, as are fit to remove the Diſeaſe,
leſt the Patient be injured by the Medicine. As
for Example, when Iron is diſſolved in *Aqua fortis*,
if you ſuddainly pour Oyl of Tartar upon that Solution, you ſhall difficultly preſerve the Glaſs from
breaking ; for the contrary Natures , like unto
Gun-powder, take Fire, and break the Glaſs. Of
all theſe Things, our Gown Doctors know nothing
at all ; therefore they have no other Defence for
their Ignorance, than Silence only.

You titular Doctors, you I ſpeak to, who write
long Scroles of Receipts : you Apothecaries, who
with your Decoctions fill Pots, no leſs than Thoſe
(in Princes Courts) in which Meat is boyled for the
ſuſtentation of ſome hundreds of men : you, I ſay,
who hitherto have been blind, ſuffer a *Collyrium* to
be poured into your Eyes, and permit them to be
anointed with Balſom, that the moſt thick skin of
Blindneſs may fall from your Sight, and you behold
the Truth, as in a moſt clear Glaſs. *G O D* grant
you

you Grace, that you may know his wonderful Works, and the Love of your Neighbour be rooted in you, that you may ſearch out true Medicine, which the Ruler of the Heavens hath, by his own omnipotent hand, and his ineffable and eternal Wiſdom, from above infuſed in, impreſſed on, and communicated to his Noble Creatures, for the Good of Mankind; whence man may find help in his greateſt Neceſſity, and Counſel for Health in his Diſeaſes. Why do you, miſerable Worm of the Earth, and food of Worms, look ſo intently on the Rind or Shell, and neglect the Kernel, being unmindful of your *Creator*, who formed you according to his Image; when as you ought to give thanks to him, and with diligent Study to ſearch out his Works, exceeding Nature her ſelf? Return and look into your ſelf, there behold the Image of your own Ingratitude, that you may be aſhamed of your ſelf, eſpecially becauſe you have not ſearched out thoſe Things, which the moſt wiſe *G O D*, for the Good of Mortals; hath infuſed in his Creatures; by knowing which, you might have offered unto him the moſt acceptable Sacrifice of Praiſe and Gratitude.

But I will put an end to this Diſcourſe, leſt my Tears (which I can ſcarcely keep in, from continually falling from mine Eyes) ſhould blot this my Writing, and whilſt I deplore the Blindneſs of the World, I blemiſh this Lamentation, which I would have known to all men. I am a man Religious, incorporated in a moſt holy Order, in which I will perſevere, as long as it ſhall pleaſe the Omnipotent *G O D*, to animate this miſerable Body with Vital Spirit: therefore I muſt not write other things, or otherwiſe, than is agreeable to this State. But had I the Office of a Secular Judge, I would lift up my Voyce, and ſound a Trumpet in their

their Ears, that thofe deaf men may hear, who hitherto would not acknowledge the Truth, but out of Ignorance, without Caufe, falfly and flande-roufly perfecute, calumniate, contemn, difparage, and meditate how they may totally fupprefs the fame.

But thou, O Lord *G O D*, who dwelleft in the Higheft, who art called and truly art the *G O D* of Reft, who fitting in the Supreme Throne of Ma-jefty, governeft Heaven and Earth, which thou haft created, who conferveft the Stars, and or-daineft the Courfe of the Firmament in its Moti-on according to thy Command, before whom all Creatures tremble, which are found in the Earth, or in Heaven, and the Infernal Spirits are aftonifh-ed with unexpreffable dread, be pleafed, I pray to look down upon the Tranfactions of this moft un-grateful World, and teach them inwardly to know thofe Things, which thou haft outwardly and vifi-bly propofed to the Sons of Men, that thou mayeft be prayfed in thy Throne, known in thy Verity, and adored in thy immenfe Majefty. As for my felf, I an unworthy and miferable man, give thanks unto thee, for thy great and infinite Gifts and Be-nefits of Riches and Health beftowed on me, and laud thy Majefty for ever for the fame. More, O my Father and Lord, I neither can, nor am able to defire in this perifhing World.

Now, that we may write of *Antimony*, and be-gin our Difcourfe from the very Foundation, whence *Antimony* acquires its Empire, Triumph and Glory, by which it is exalted to perfect Opera-tion, we muft before all Things difcover the cer-tain Original of its Root: how it is generated in the Earth, to the Dominion of what Stars it is fub-jected, and what Elements have throughly dige-fted it, and which they be, that have brought it to Maturity.

Maturity. *Antimony* is no other than a Fume, or
(as I may otherwife call it) a Mineral Vapour,
which is genited from above by the Stars, and afterward by the Elements deduced and digefted to
formal Coagulation and Maturity. Here it is to
be noted, that *Antimony* hath acquired its Effence,
Virtue, Power, Operation and Quality, from the
fame Principle, Root and Effence, whence Vulgar
Mercury is produced; yet with more firm Coagulation, fo that it is brought to an harder Effence,
than the living or running Mercury of the Vulgar
hath. The Reafon of this is, becaufe it hath affumed from the three Principles, a little more of the
Subftance of Salt, than Conimon Mercury. For
although of all the three Principles, it hath the
leaft part of Salt, yet it hath affumed more of the
Effence of Salt, than common Mercury, whence unto it hath hapned fuch a Coagulation. Hardnefs
in every thing is from Salt, which vulgar Mercury
hath not. For it hath a very fmall part of Salt,
but in it, in a fpiritual manner, is inhted a certain
more hot *Spirit* of *Sulphur*; therefore it alwayes
flows, and cannot be brought to Coagulation, unlefs by the help of other Metallick Spirits, which
endued with very great Virtues, are chiefly found
in the *Matrix* of *Saturn*, without which it cannot
be fixed, unlefs by him, who poffeffeth the *Stone* of
Philofophers, by which its three Principles may be
brought to a concordant Equality, and then it acquires fuch a Body, as will melt, flow, and abide the
Hammer, like all other Metals: otherwife Mercury is and will be fluid Mercury, until its volatility be
this way taken away. Hence it is known, that all
Animals and all Vegetables are too weak to fix Mercury into a malleable Subftance (as many have in
va'n endeavoured) becaufe all thefe have not a Metallick Nature. *Mercury*, within and without, is

no

no other than meer Fire; therefore it is not com-
buſtible by any Fire, no Fire can apprehend it ſo;
as to alter its Eſſence, but it ſuddenly flies and reſolves it ſelf into an incombuſtible Oyl Spiritually;
or after its fixation it remains ſo invariable, as no
ſtrength or power of men is ſufficient again to alter it. And whatſoever can now be made of Gold
may then alſo be made of it by Art; becauſe after
Coagulation it is altogether like Gold: for it with
Gold hath one and the ſame Root, Stock, or Production originally.

But ſince I purpoſe not in this place to diſcourſe
more largely of *Mercury*, and intend only ſimply
(yet truly) to deſcribe the very Foundation of *Antimony*, from true and certain Principles, I will ceaſe
to ſpeak of *Mercury*, and proceed to a further Declaration of *Antimony*. Yet, whatſoever I have
propoſed by way of Similitude touching *Mercury* *;
for an Introduction and further Conſideration, is
not written in vain, or to no purpoſe; but to the
end, that the very Beginning of *Antimony* may be
more clearly underſtood, which (as I before ſhewed)
received its original, as it were Mercurially, with
it.

* *which ſo miſerably perplexeth all the Students of this Art: what our*
Mercury *is, which is the Matter of the Stone, which is found every where*
and in all Things, is here briefly and clearly manifeſted. Therefore our Author
Baſilius *doth not in Vain invite your Attention. All the Light I am able to*
add to this Clearneſs, would rather obſcure, than illuſtrate the ſame: therefore,
with him, I admoniſh you to attend.

Wherefore moſt diligently think on this; often
bear in mind, obſerve and underſtand, that all Minerals and Metals together, in the ſame Time, and
after the ſame manner, and of one and the ſame
principal Matter, are produced and genited.
That Matter is no other, than a meer Vapour;

which

which is extracted from the Elementary Earth by
the Superior *Stars*, as by a Sydereal Diftillation of
the Macrocofm: which Sydereal hot Infufion, with
an Airy-Sulphureous Property defcending upon Inferiors, fo acts and operates, as in thofe Metals and
Minerals is implanted fpiritually and invifibly a
certain Power and Virtue, which Fume afterward
refolves it felf in the Earth, into a certain Water,
from which Mineral Water all Metals are thenceforth generated and ripened to their Perfection;
and thence proceeds this or that Metal or Mineral, according as one of the three Principles acquires Dominion, and they have much or little of
Sulphur and Salt, or an unequal Mixture of the
weight of them, whence fome Metals are fixed;
that is, fome conftant and ftable, fome volatile and
eafily mutable, as is feen in *Gold, Silver, Copper, Iron,
Tin* and *Lead.* Befides thefe Metals, other Minerals alfo are generated of the three Principles, according to the Communication and Participation
of the unequal weight of them: as are *Vitriol, Antimony*, and many other Marchafites, or other E-
lectrums, and Minerals, which for brevity fake we
here omit.

But Gold, in its *Aftrum* and Beginning was imbibed with a much more perfect *Sulphur*, and a
much more perfect *Mercury*, than all other Metals
and Minerals, and therefore its operative Virtue is
much more potent and more efficacious, than the
Aftrums of other Metals : Yea, all Virtues whatfoever are difperfed in other Metals, and many more
than them, are found in the *Aftrum* of Gold only.
Moreover I fay, when that one thing is brought to
further Maturity by Fire, it contains more Perfection, than all Metals and Minerals together. There
is one only Mineral, of which I have often made
mention already, in which is found a Sulphur of

Sol,

Sol, equally as ſtrong and powerful, yea more potent and more ſtrong, than in Gold it ſelf: ſo alſo,
there are two kinds of Metals found, in which this
Predominancy powerfully Triumphs, of which at
this time I have neither will nor diſpoſition to
write; but I am willing to keep within the Bounds
I have ſet my ſelf in treating of the Eſſence of *Antimony*, touching which I purpoſe now to ſpeak.

Therefore *Antimony* is a Mineral made of the
Vapour of the Earth changed into Water, which
Spiritual Syderal Tranſmutation is the true *Aſtrum*
of *Antimony*; which Water, by the Stars firſt, afterward by the Element of Fire, which reſides in
the Element of Air, is extracted from the Elementary Earth, and by Coagulation formally changed
into a tangible Eſſence, in which tangible Eſſence,
(*viz.* whence *Antimony* is formally made) is found
very much of *Sulphur* predominant, of *Mercury*
not ſo much, and of *Salt* the leaſt of all three; yet
it aſſumes ſo much *Salt*, as it thence acquires an
hard and immalleable Maſs. The principal Quality of it is dry and hot, or rather burning, of Cold
and Humidity it hath very little in it, as there is in
Common Mercury; in Corporal Gold alſo is more
Heat than Cold. Theſe may ſuffice to be ſpoken
of the Matter, and three Fundamental Principles of
Antimony, how by the *Archeus* in the Element of
Earth it is brought to perfection.

Yet the Lovers of *Chymiſtry* ſhould not think
this Philoſophick Reaſon by me alleadged of ab-
ſolute neceſſity to them, nor need they be ſolici-
tous to know, in what Center the *Aſtrum* of *Antimony* reſts, or from what Root it flows; but ſhould
rather deſire to learn the Utility and uſe thereof;
viz. which way it ought to be prepared and reduced to its State, that they may know its Virtue,
Power, and Operation, touching which in times

paſt ſo many Things have been written, and to this Day are mentioned, and ſpoken of by all men of all States and Conditions. For the Learned, as well as the Unlearned hope to have their ardent and inſatiable Deſire ſatisfied by This; therefore I will not detain the Reader with ambiguous Diſcourſes, or tedious Delays, but ſimply teach every Thing, which I by great Study and Diligence (which I have often imployed about *Antimony*) could find out touching the Eſſence of *Antimony*. For no man, by reaſon of the ſhortneſs of Life, can know or ſearch out all its *Arcanum*'s: becauſe in Preparation of *Antimony*, one new Wonder follows another perpetually; one Degree ſucceeds a former Degree, Colour follows Colour, and one Virtue, Power or Operation always manifeſts it ſelf greater than another.

And, to begin here I ſay, *Antimony* is meer Venom, not of the kind of the leaſt Venoms, but ſuch, as by which you may deſtroy Men and Beaſts, ſo venomous a power is diffuſed through the whole Subſtance of this Mineral. Hence ariſeth the common Exclamation of all men. For the People, unskilful Doctors, and all Thoſe, to whom the ground of true Medicine is unknown, do with one mouth proclaim it *Venom*, *Venom* ! Poyſon, ſay they (as I my ſelf above confeſſed) lies in *Antimony*. For this Cauſe let us diſſwade all men from its uſe; for it endangers the Health and Life. Therefore *Doctors* reſident in Princes Courts, admoniſh Monarchs, Princes, and other Potentates not to uſe *Antimony*. Other Scholaſticks cry out, Beware, you in no wiſe admit *Antimony* into Medicinal Uſe ; for it's meer Poyſon: theſe the Inhabitants of Cities and Villages follow. And this far ſpread Clamour ſo moves the greateſt part of Mortals, as *Antimony* in theſe our Days is very ill ſpoken of, and no

man

man dares put confidence in the Medicine thereof, which in it is found so various and unexpressible. For truly and holily I affirm (as truly as *GOD* is the Creator of all things visible, which are contained in Heaven or Earth, which either have come, or in time to come shall come unto our knowledge) that under Heaven, or by the Rays of the Sun, with the Guidance of Experience, can be found or demonstrated no greater Medicine, than is in this Mineral; yea, there is no Subject, in which so fluently and abundantly can be found such most certain Remedies for Health, as shall be declared (by sure and undeniable Experiments) to be in *Antimony*.

Son, attend to this my Discourse, and do thou Reader give heed to my Writings, and do you wise men of the World diligently observe my Declaration of *Antimony* founded on Experience. For my *Theory* ariseth from Nature, and my *Practice* proceeds from certain Experience, which shews its manifold Utility, and infinite Ways produceth the same, not without the incredible Admiration of all men. But I assent to you, and confess (as I have before acknowledged in my Writings) that *Antimony* at first is meer Venom, and before Preparation hath nothing in or with it self, but Poyson; and that I affirm to be true. But you, whosoever you are, insignized or not insignized with the Degree of *Doctor*, *Master*, or *Batcheler*, whether skilful in Art, or by some other Priviledge promoted; you, I say, who so inconsiderately and so arrogantly without Truth exclaim, and prate against me, pause a while, and forget not your own Argument, hear what I have here to say. *Antimony* is Venom, therefore every One must beware he use it not. No, that doth not follow Mr. *Doctor*, *Batchelor*, or *Master*; it doth not follow, I say, Mr. *Doctor*,

although

although you be proud of your Red Hat. *Treacle* is made of the moſt perillous Venom of a *Viper*, which is called Ὀήελον,whence alſo it had its Name ; therefore no man muſt uſe it, for there is poyſon in it. Doth this Conſequence pleaſe you? How doth this my Doctrine like you? You hear, that after Preparation, no Venenoſity is found in *Anti-mony*; for by the Spagyrick Art *Antimony* is con-verted from Venom into Medicine, no otherwiſe than as of the Venom of a Viper is ſaid, which is con-verted into *Treacle*; but without Preparation you ſhall find no Good in it, nor any thing of Medici-nal Help, but much loiſ and detriment.

Now, whoſoever deſires to become a Diſciple of *Antimony*, he muſt, after Prayer, and an earneſt Invocation of *G O D*, betake himſelf to the School of *Vulcan*; for he is the Maſter and Revealer of all Secrets. This Maſter is contemned by the Wiſe Men of the World, ſet very light by and derided; becauſe they, by reaſon of their own Negligence and Malignity, have learned nothing of him; and all Revelation, through their own Sloath, is impe-ded : for no Medicine was ever prepared without *Vulcan*, whatſoever thoſe ſenſleſs mad men ſhall bable and affirm to the Contrary.

But I will proceed to the Proceſs and Preparati-on of *Antimony*; for I little value the Clamours of arrogant and ſelf applauding men : let them make and bring to light any Work that can excel *Anti-mony*. It is well known to me, that of *Antimony* may be made Medicines equal to Thoſe, which are in Gold and vulgar Mercury (I except the *Aſtrum of Sol*) for of this may be prepared *Aurum potabile* againſt the Leproſie, of this may be made Spirit of Mercury, the higheſt Remedy againſt the French *P O X*, of this other infinite Remedies may be pre-pared. If thoſe Contemners cannot perceive and

underſtand

underſtand this, what wonder is it? None, becauſe they have not learned it. No man can give a ſound Judgment of that, which he never learned. Let the Aſs, an *Animal* like them in ſtupidity be their Example, who cannot teach a Shepherd how to handle his Pipe, ſo as to play an Harmonious Tune ; becauſe he hath not learned. So, right Judgement, with a ſolid Foundation cannot be given by a man, who before hath not bent his Studies that way, that from Writings he may be able to diſcern what, in ſuch a Buſineſs, is juſt or unjuſt. After the ſame manner in this Faculty, what can be attributed to any of the *Doctors*, before he hath from Writings, and by his own proper labour acquired Knowledge?

Yet before I paſs to the Proceſs it ſelf, ſome One may perhaps interrupt and ask me, which way both Minerals and other Things receive their Venenoſity? What Venom is? Whence the Poyſon of every Thing hath its Original? How it may be taken away, alſo how ſuch a Mineral may without peril ſecurely be uſed for Health after evacuation of that Venom? To theſe Queſtions I will briefly and clearly anſwer. The Infuſion of Venom falls under a twofold Conſideration, *viz.* Natural and Supernatural.

The firſt Reaſon, why *G O D* the ſupreme Lord of the Stars, and the Maker of Heaven and Earth, hath propoſed to us open Venom, eſpecially in Minerals, is, that by this his Ordination he might ſhew to us his Wonders and powerful Works, for diſtinction of Good and Evil, as in the Law he preſcribed to us the Knowledge of That, which lies as a Duty on us to do, *viz.* to Chooſe the Good and Eſchew the Evil. So alſo the Tree of Life in Paradiſe was propoſed ; its right uſe tended to Good, but its abuſe brought the Fall to Evil ; for by

E 4 that

that *GOD*'s Command was broke, whence procced-
ed Deſtruction and all Evil. This is the firſt Reaſon.

A Second Reaſon is, that by this we might comprehend and underſtand the Diſtinction between
Evil and Good, and at length learn to exterminate
Malice and repoſit Goodneſs in its place. For
GOD wills not , that man ſhould periſh and be de-
ſtroyed, but that he ſhould depart from Evil, and
come to amendment of Life, that Deſtruction may
be driven far away from his Soul. So, to Us his
Creatures, with wonderful Conveniency hath he
propoſed Good and Evll, which is found both in the
Precept of the Word, aud in the Work of the Creature; that we may chooſe what is profitable and good
for Health, and ſhun what is evil and pernitious.

Thirdly, Venom is alſo made by the Stars, when
contrary Oppoſitions and Conjunctions of them
happen, by which the Elements are Infected ſo, as
they become the Cauſe of Peſtilences, and other
Venomous Diſeaſes in this World : which alſo is
to be underſtood of *Comets*.

Fourthly, Venom is made from Things repugnant each to other, as when any One inkindles a
deadly Poyſon in himſelf, by Anger or Sadneſs;
alſo when a man drinks being above meaſure hot.

Fifthly, among Venoms may be numbred Wea-
pons, with which any One is ſlain ; then the Abuſe
of Arms is Venom to that man. But when any One
uſeth Arms, for the juſt and unblamable defence of
his Body, to which end they were invented, then
they may be accounted a certain kind of Medicine.

Laſtly, the Cauſe of Venom may be demonſtrated
by Nature, in this manner : whatſoever Nature reſiſts is Venom, and that becauſe it fights againſt Nature. As when any one eats ſuch Food, as his *Stomach* cannot bear, then that Food is Venom to him ;
for it is repugnant to Nature : on the contrary,

if

if any One eat such Food, as is Friendly to his Stomach, to him that Food is Medicine.

But Venom is principally attracted to Bodies in the Earth, whilst they are a certain Mercurial Essence (now I speak of the Venom of Minerals) which yet is in an immature, crude, and not well digested Form, which is repugnant to Nature, and difficultly digested; because such a Mercurial Essence is not yet perfect, well digested to Maturity, therefore it passeth through the whole Body, as a crude, immature, undigestible Mineral. As if crude Corn should be eaten by men, that would be so difficult to be digested by the Stomach, as a notable debility of the Body would follow. For the natural Heat is too weak to deduce that to a due Concoction and Perfection. Corn, which receives its Maturity from the Fire of the Great World, must afterward be throughly cocted by the Minor Fire, that it may be digested by the Microcosm. As before we said, touching the boyling of Flesh to Maturity; so here the same is to be understood of *Antimony*, which being yet crude, and not throughly cocted in the Earth to fixedness, the Stomach of Man (as I may so speak) is too weak to bear it, or retain the same, as by certain Experience is manifested, *viz.* that all *Catharticks*, whether Minerals, Animals or Vegetables, are venomous, because of a certain Mercurial volatile Matter still predominant in them; which volatile Spirit is the Cause why other things, which are in man, are expelled: not that by this Means the Root it self of Diseases is laid hold on, which only is effected by the fixedness of every Medicine. For every Medicine throughly fixed, searcheth out fixed Diseases, and eradicates them; which Purgers not fixed cannot do, but they do only as it were carry away some Spoyl from Diseases; or they may be
compared

compared to Water which driven by force through
a Street Penetrates not the Earth it ſelf. Fixed
Remedies purge not by the Inferior Parts, becauſe
that is not the familiar way of Expelling fixed
Venoms, and that way they would not touch the
Kernel (as I may call it or Center of the Diſeaſe;
but by expelling Sweat, and otherways they ſtrike
at the very inmoſt Root of the Diſeaſe, not contented with a certain ſuperficial Expulſion of Filths.
Therefore we often admoniſh all and every One,
that all venomous Impurity is totally to be taken
away from *Antimony*, before it can either be, or be
called ſuch a Medicine, as may ſafely be given. For
this Cauſe, the Good muſt be ſeparated from the
Evil, the Fixed from the not fixed, and the Medicine from the Venom with accurate diligence, if
we hope by the Uſe of *Antimony* to obtain true
Honour, and true Utility; but Fire only can effect that. For *Vulcan* is the ſole and only Maſter
of all Theſe. Whatſoever the *Vulcan* in the Greater Orbe leaves crude and perfects not, that in the
Leſſer World muſt be amended by a certain other
Vulcan, ripning the Immature, and cocting the
Crude by Heat, and ſeparating the Pure from the
Impure. That this is poſſible no man doubts; for
dayly Experience teacheth the ſame, and it is very
apparent in the Corporal Aſpect of Colours, which
proceed from the Fire. For by Separation and
Fire, which perfect Fixation, Venenoſity is taken
away, and a Change is made of the Evil into Good,
as we have already ſaid. Therefore Fire is the
Separator of Venom from Medicine, and of Good
from Evil; which is a thing, that None of the *Phy-*
ſicians either dares or can truly and fundamentally
own, or demonſtrate to me, unleſs he who hath
firmly contracted Friendſhip with *Vulcan*, and inſtituted the ſiry Bath full of Love, by which the
Spouſe,

Spoufe, being throughly purged from all Defilement, may legitimately lie down with her Bridegroom in the Marriage Bed.

Fie upon the Acutenefs of the Worldly Wit of thofe, who neither underftand, nor are willing to endeavour to underftand thefe my Writings. If you did know, what is called fixed, and what not fixed, and what it fignifies to feparate the Pure from the Impure, affuredly you would purpofely forget many Things, and omitting other vain Works, would follow me only. For in me (*Antimony* fpeaks of himfelf) you will find *Mercury, Sulphur* and *Salt,* then which Nothing is more Conducible for the Health of men. *Mercury* is in the *Regulus, Sulphur* in the Red Colour, and *Salt* in the remaining black Earth. He that can feparate thefe, and again unite them in a due manner, according to Art, fo as Fixation may bear Rule, without Venom, he may rejoyce with Honour and Truth; becaufe he hath obtained the *Stone* of *Fire*, which may be prepared of *Antimony* for the Health of Mortals, and for Temporal Suftentation with particular profit. For in *Antimony* you may find all Colours, Black, White, Red, Green, Blew, Yellow, and more other mixt Colours, than can be believed, all which may be feparated apart, and known particularly, and fingularly applied to ufe; according as the Artift intends, fuch an Ordination is to be inftituted.

Therefore now will I diftinctly declare, how Medicine is to be prepared, Venom to be expelled, Fixation to be fet about, and a true Separation to be made, by which the Evil may be fubdued and depreffed, and the Good triumph and be taken into ufe. In the mean while, let the Lover of Art confider, that every of the other Metals may be compared to every of the Pretious Stones; but this only contains univerfally the Virtues of all Stones;

which

which thofe Colours, which it gives forth and ex-
hibits to the Sight from it felf in the Fire, do fufficiently demonftrate. Its Tranfparent Rednefs is
affigned to the Carbuncle, Ruby, and Coral; its
Whitenefs, to the Diamond and Cryftal; its
Blew Colour, to the *Saphire*; Green, to the *Em-*
rald; Yellow, to the *Jacinth*; its Black, to the
Granate, which Stone contains in it felf a certain
Blacknefs occultly abfconded. But as to Metals,
the Black is affigned to *Saturn*, the Red to Iron, the
Yellow to Gold, the Green to Copper, the Blew
to Silver, the White to *Mercury*, and its mixture
of various Colours is attributed to *Jupiter*. But
as all the Colours of all Metals and Precious Stones
are clearly found in *Antimony*; fo alfo all the powers and Virtues of Medicine are no lefs fhewed in
it, than the Colours aforefaid : but to educe from
it all thefe Colours is not the Labour of one man.
For our Life is circumfcribed with Limits more
ftrait, than will permit one man by his Labour
throughly to learn whatfoever Nature keeps concealed and abfconded in her Bofom. In one certain way of Preparation, from *Antimony* by diftil-
lations is drawn forth an Humour acid and fharp,
like true perfect Vinegar. Another way is prepared a fhining Red Colour, fweet and favoury, as purified Honey or Sugar. Another way, a Worm-
wood-liike Bitternefs proceeds therefrom; otherwife, a certain Acrimony, like fome Salt-Oyl : thus
always one Nature follows another. Again, by
Sublimation it is driven to the Olympick Mountains, like a flying Eagle, red, yellow and white.
Alfo forced down by Defcent, it yields divers Colours and Preparations : alfo by Reverberation,
of it is made a Metal, like common Lead. Likewife a tranfparent Glafs, red, yellow, white, black,
and endewed with other Colours : all which notwithftanding,

withstanding, are not safe to be used in Medicine, unless they be first proved by another *Examen*. Also it is resolved into rare and wonderful Oyls, which are various and manifold, some of which are made perfect with Addition, others without mixtion of any other things; some likewise are taken inwardly, others only outwardly applied to common Ulcers, and Wounds. It supplies us with so many several Extractions, varied with so many Colours, as it would tire a *Delphian Apollo* to describe them all; but indeed, all the Mutations of its Nature, which are discovered through the Gate of Fire, it by its own Oracles will best unfold. Of it is made living Mercury, and Sulphur which burns like common Sulphur, so that of that Gunpowder might be made. Of it is made a true and natural *Salt*; and many other things are prepared of the same.

Therefore we begin to speak of the Preparations thereof, as of its *Essence*, *Magistery*, *Arcanum*, *Elixir*, and particular *Tincture*, in which you must imploy all diligence and Care; especially when I shall in my Writings declare to you the Stone of Fire, and its Preparation, together with other various Secrets and Arcanums, which indeed are scarcely at all known to the World; and which have been little regarded, since the *Egyptians*, *Arabians* and *Chaldeans* dyed, who professed these Arts: of which notwithstanding the use is very great, for searching out the very Fountain of true Medicine, and all other Works pertinent thereunto.

Now diligently mind, and with profound Meditation consider all the following Preparations, one succeeding another, as I shall reveal them. For there is no One inserted, which hath not its singular Utility, but every of them is useful, according as ordained in its State. A fixed Medicine of *Antimony*,

timony, expels fixed Difeafes and eradicates them;
but *Antimony* not fixed, as when it is crude and not
prepared, opens and purgeth the Stomach only,
but toucheth not the Root of the Difeafe. Therefore I will fet about the Preparation of all, that appertains to *Antimony*, and difcover all the Keys of
its Preparation, which now (as by a new Nativity)
are brought to Light, and revealed by Fire, in the
fame ftate, to which they were ordained by *G O D*
their *Creator*. This unlocking and preparing of
Mineral *Antimony* is performed by divers Methods
and Ways, by the difpofure and governance of the
Fire, with manifold labour of the Hands, whence
proceeds the Operation, Virtue, Power and Colour of the Medicine it felf. And fince *Antimony*
to the Afpect prefents a crude black Colour, mixed
with a little whitenefs, I will firft fpeak of its de-
ftructive alteration, which confifts in *Calcination* and
Incineration, and that is thus made.

Take Hungarian or other *Antimony*, the beft
you can get, grind it, if poffible, to an Impalpable
Powder; this Powder fpread Thin all over the
Bottom of a Calcining Pan, round or fquare,
which hath a Rim round about, the height of two
Fingers thicknefs; fet this Pan into a Calcining
Fornace, and adminifter to it at firft a very moderate
Fire of Coals, which afterward increafe gradually:
when you fee a Fume beginning to arife from the
Antimony, ftir it continually with an Iron *Spatula*,
without ceafing, as long as it wall give forth from
it felf any Fume. If in Calcining, the *Antimony*
melt, or concrete into Clots, then remove it from
the Fire, and when cold again reduce it to a fubtle
Powder, and as before calcine it, continually ftir-
ring as we faid, until no more Fume will afcend.
If need be repeat this Operation fo often and fo
long, as until that *Antimony* put into the Fire, will
neither

neither fume, nor concrete into Clots, but in Colour refemble White and pure Afhes : Then is the Calcination of *Antimony* rightly made.

Put this *Antimony* thus calcined into a Goldfmiths Crucible fet in a Fornace, and urge the Fire with Bellows, or put it into a Wind-Fornace, adminiftring fuch Fire, as the *Antimony* may flow, like clear and pure Water. Then, that you may certainly and infallibly prove , whether the Glafs made thereof be fufficiently cocted, and hath acquired a tranfparent Colour, put a long rod of Iron cold into the Crucible, and part of the Glafs will ftick to the Iron, which with an Hammer ftrike off, and hold up againft the Light, to fee whether it be clear, clean and tranfparent ; if fo, it is well, and perfectly mature.

Here let my Reader, unlearned and but a Beginner in Art, know (for I write not to men skilled in this Art, who have often experienced the powers of the Fire, but to Candidates, *Tyro*'s, * and the ftudious Difciples of the *Spagyrick* Science ; becaufe to make Glafs of *Antimony* is a thing common, and well known to many) know, I fay, that every Glafs, whether made of Metals, Minerals, or any other Matter, muft be throughly cocted in Fire to due Maturity, that it may have a clear and tranfparent Colour, and be apt for further Preparation to Medicinal ufe : which tranflucid and pure Maturity *Vulcan* only effects in his fecret and hidden Nature. Therefore, let every man know, confider and retain this.

When

ries. *For me, let every One pleaſe himſelf in his own Writings: ſurely I think I have offered ſomewhat, which Poſterity will always thankfully accept. For although I did for ſeveral years moſt diligently read* Baſilius *and other Maſters of the Art of Arts, and in Labouring followed them, as exactly as poſſibly I could, yet I committed ſo many Errors (the remembrance of which fills me with Horror) loſt ſo much Money, and was ſo often conſtrained to amend thoſe Errors with labour, as I have compaſſion of all Thoſe, who would enter into this way, incited thereunto by their earneſt deſire to help their Neighbours: for I have no reſpect to Others, who aim at nothing but Riches, and would make ſo noble an Art ſubſervient to* Avarice, *the worſt of all Vices; let them ſuſtain the dammage they deſerve to ſuffer. But do you, who are endued with a more noble* Spirit, *Firſt ſeek the Kingdom of* GOD, *which is either conſtituted or propagated by Charity to your Neighbour, and all other Things, which other men ſo impiouſly ſeek, ſhall ſpontaneouſly (which is the Bounty of* GOD) *be added to you. I need to uſe no great Arguments to perſwade any man to read thoſe Commentaries; for every One's own Buſineſs will ſufficiently admoniſh him, when he ſhall ſee me often with one word, and a moſt ſimple Animadverſion to ſave him ſo great Charges, which he hath too frequently beſtowed in labouring without ſucceſs. I do here candidly profeſs to thee, ſtudious Reader, had the Manual Operations been as ſincerely ſhewed to me, as I here open them, I ſhould have ſaved a great Sum of Money; for I very often erred, when I would over eagerly proſecute certain* Proceſſes *of others, and by that vain endeavour, loſt ſome Thouſands of* Florens. *Yet I ſeldome twice repeated any of theſe Operations, which our Author (moſt ſincerely and openly, of all that I know) hath in this Book inſerted. I ſhall not here inſtitute a Tyrocinium of* Chymiſtry, *as other Authors, well known to young Beginners, have already done; but I am willing, by Admonition to help thoſe, who long ſince could looſe this Subject from its Bonds, and with moſt fervent deſire deſign to arive to the Goal expoſed to their Eyes and Mind, leaſt either ſlippery Blood in the way, or* Entellus *now lying proſtrate, ſhould hinder them from gaining the propoſed Reward, which is* Riches *and* Health.

When in the Method we have taught, your *Antimony* is converted into Glaſs, take a Platter or Diſh made of Copper, which is ſmooth and broad, heat it hot at the Fire, otherwiſe your Matter will flie out; then pour in the fluid Matter as thin as you can, and you will have pure, yellow, tranſparent Glaſs of *Antimony*. This is the beſt way of preparing Glaſs of *Antimony per ſe*, without addition; and this Glaſs, above all others, is endewed with the greateſt Virtue and Power, which it manifeſts

nifests after its further Preparation. This is by
me called *Pure* Glaſs of *Antimony.* *

> * *This is now the Common, and well known way of making Glaß of Anti-*
> *mony, which is profitable in many Operations : but to adminiſter it ſo to the*
> *Sick without Diſtinction, is a Work full of danger and peril. It indeed ſuc-*
> *ceeds happily, but this caſual or accidental health of ſome, is not of ſo great mo-*
> *ment, as therefore to expoſe the Life of one man to Peril. For I have ſeen a Sick*
> *man, who after he had taken but half an ounce of the Infuſion, vomited and*
> *purged above meaſure, and ſoon after died. Hence are thoſe Tears, hence thoſe*
> *Clamours ariſe againſt* Chymiſts, *as if the impious raſhneß of ſome falſe Chy-*
> *miſts were to be imputed to the Art, which* Pſeudochymiſts *care not how many*
> *Houſes they fill with Funerals, provided one or two that are healed will blaze*
> *their Fame, and they can bear themſelves called* Doctors, *and rob the ſimple of*
> *their money. The reaſon of this great danger is, becauſe all the Emetick force*
> *of* Antimony *contained in the fixed Salt thereof, in which reſides all its Vene-*
> *noſity, which weak Natures cannot overcome, and therefore receive not ſo much*
> *good from the Salutiferous virtue thereof, as hurt from its Venom. But this*
> *thing ſhould not deter ſound men from the uſe of* Antimony, *ſince they ſee it,*
> *even then when mixed with Venom, often to produce ſalutary Effects. They*
> *ſhould rather thus reaſon : if that ſalutiferous Virtue be freed from the Noxious*
> *faculty, what Good would it not do, or what Diſeaſes would it not heal?*
> *Therefore, behold I here offer to you ſuch Glaß of Antimony, as I my ſelf uſe*
> *often, and may be uſed by every man, without any danger of a mortal Cata-*
> *trophe.*
>
> *Take pure Glaß of Antimony, made as* Baſilius *here teacheth, melt it in a*
> *Crucible, and keep it in flux ſo long, as until a third part be conſumed. Then*
> *let it cool, and grind the ſame to an Impalpable Powder, upon which pour Spi-*
> *rit of Wine highly rectified, until it ſtand three fingers above the Powder;*
> *cloſe the Veſſel firmly, and circulate the Matter for three Moneths; then by*
> *Diſtillation abſtract the Spirit of Wine, or if it be tinged with Redneß, (which*
> *always will be, if you have rightly operated) only pour it off, and keep it apart,*
> *or it is an excellent Medicine. The remaining Body put into a Crucible, per-*
> *mit it to flow, and then caſt it into what Forms you will. For it can aſſume*
> *whatſoever Shapes you will have it, which may be ſet in Rings, and worn on*
> *the Hand. But its Medicinal uſe is thus.*
>
> *Put this Glaß for one Night in two ounces of Cold Wine, and in the Morning*
> *let the Sick drink that Wine, and you will find very good ſucceſs; for it purg-*
> *eth kindly, and if Nature incline to bring the Matter upward, it performs that*
> *action moderately, cauſing gentle Vomits. Only Note this : the preſcribed Doſe*
> *muſt be diminiſhed, according to the Strength, Age and Conſtitution of the Sick.*
> *Here, Reader, candidly accept of this my firſt Admonition offered to thy ſelf,*
> *and expect to find more, if you willingly and intently peruſe the after follow-*
> *ing.*

E   For

For there are other Glaffes prepared of *Antimo-ny*, by Addition of *Borax* and other things, in this manner.

Take of Crude *Antimony* one part, of *Venetian Borax* two parts; put thefe together into a Cruci-ble, which fetting the Veffel in a Wind-Fornace, or urging the Fire with Bellows, caufe to flow, that they may be well and perfectly mixed toge-ther, afterward pour out the Mixture into a Pan, or Difh of Copper made hot, as thin as is poffible, as before was faid in the Superior Preparation, and you will find your *Antimony* fair and tranfparently clear, *like a *Pyropus* or Ruby, provided you ob-ferve the due and accurate Method, Operating as you ought, in Governing the Fire.

* *The Caution, to which our* Author *here afcribes the Succefs, is that you ufe a moft ftrong Fire, fuch as is required for melting of Gold : for without this you cannot acquire the Rednefs of a* Pyropus.

The Rednefs may be abftracted from this Red Glafs, with Spirit of Wine *, and by long conti-nued Circulation in Fire, be perfected, and rendred a moft excellent, profitable and efficacious Medi-cine.

* *Not with common Spirit of wine, but with Philofophick Spirit, which for extracting this Tincture, I thus prepare.*
Take of Sal-Armoniack thrice fublimed $\mathfrak{Z}$iiij. Spirit of wine, diftilled up-on Salt of Tartar fo, as it may be perfectly dephlegmated : put them together in a Phial, which place it in heat of Digeft on the Spirit may fully imbibe the Sulphur or Fire of the Sal-Armoniack ; then diftil the mixture by Alembick thrice, and you will have a true Menftruum, wherewith to Extract that Rednefs from the Glafs of Antimony.
Alfo the Tincture of this Glafs is extracted with its proper Vinegar, and by a further Operation is perfected, and becomes a moft excellent Medicament.

But a tranfparent white Glafs of *Antimony*, af-ter commixtion thereof, is prepared in this man-ner.   Take

Take *Antimony* beat or ground small one part; *Venetian Borax* very pure four parts: put these, well mixed together, into a Crucible, and cause the Mixture to flow well. At first indeed it will be yellow, but if it stand longer in Fire, the yellowness vanisheth, the Matter receives a white Colour, and thenceforth becomes a fair and white Glass. Whether this Colour be brought to perfect Maturity, you may prove with a cold Iron, as above is said. Many other ways of *Antimony* may be formed Glasses * consisting almost of Infinite Forms.

* *Let him who desires to prepare more Glasses of* Antimony, *consult De-guinus,* Hartman, Crollius, *and other Authors ; we here acquiesce in these proposed by* Basilius.

But since my purpose here was not to describe other Glasses, then I my self had experienced, and which manifest happy success in Healing, I judged it unnecessary to waste Paper in describing them, or by a tedious discourse to weary the Reader ; especially since, unto you is already in part proposed the principal Colour *(viz.* the Red) which is found in Glass made of *Antimony.* The black Colour, which *Antimony* had before Preparation, is now in a Spiritual manner flown up the Chimney ; because in such a Spiritual manner, very much of the Venomous Substance had left it before, through the Expulsive force of the Fire, as by Calcination. Yet because in this Preparation all the whole Venom is not taken away from the Glass of *Antimony*, but it still retains very much thereof; I am willing (now I have begun) further to reveal to you, which way the Venom may wholly be removed from this Glass, and another Separation of the Pure from the Impure, of the Venom from the Medicine, be instituted ; by which the Tongue of the *Orator* will be loosed, and occasion given to him of largely

expres-

expreſſing my Praiſes , and publiſhing the ſame, as
with a great Sound, through all Parts of this Inferiour Orb: which will be a neceſſary Conſequence
of the Gratitude of my Diſciples, when they ſhall
ſee with their Eyes, touch with their Hands, and
with their Underſtanding comprehend , that I to
their great profit, have declared to them the very
Truth, withour Deceit, and made them the Heirs
of a memorable Teſtament.

Therefore the firſt Separation of the Sulphure
from its Body, and the Extraction of the Tincture
from its Salt, is performed in this manner.   Take
pure Glaſs of *Antimony*, as I taught you to make it,
without the adjunction of any other Thing, Grind
it to ſubtle Powder * impalpable as Flower ;

*What I here ſhall adviſe is ſhort , but very profitable , without which
what the Author appoints cannot be done, nor by beating or grinding in a Mortar can you ever bring the Body to a requiſite fineneſs, much leſs upon a Porphyry
Stone can you grind the ſame.   Therefore firſt beat it in a Mortar, afterward
mix it with diſtilled Vinegar, that it may have the Conſiſtency of a ſoft Pap-
like matter, and ſo grind it upon a Porphyry Stone, as Painters grind their Colours, and undoubtedly you will obtain your deſire.*

Which Powder put into a Glaſs with a Plain flat
bottom, called a Cucurbit, and there pour upon it
ſtrong Vinegar well rectified: then ſet the Veſſel in
a Digeſtive Fire, or if it be Summer, expoſe it to
the Sun, ſtirring it twice or thrice * a Day, and ſo
long digeſt it in that temperate heat , as until the
Vinegar contract a Yellow Colour inclining to Redneſs, like the Colour of moſt clean and well purified Gold.

* *Thou art happy, if thou canſt be wiſe by my Dammage, O Lover of Art.
I exactly followed this ſhort Admonition, ſtirring the Cucurbit twice or thrice
a Day, but the Matter was alwvys coagulated like a Stone, and ſtuck ſo firmly
to the bottom , as it could by no force be removed thence: but afterward, being
h . . .*

Then

more wary, from the very first I begun to stir the Matter with a Wooden Spatula five or six times a Day, or oftner ; you may imitate the same, if you be wise, not only here, but also in the Superior Preparation of Antimony , and in every Extraction of Tincture from Antimony.

Then pour off this clear and pure Extraction, and pour on fresh Vinegar, and repeat the Operation, as long as the Vinegar is tinged, and until no more Tincture can be extracted. Filter all these Extractions mix'd together, and put them into a Glaſs Body, with its Head annexed, and by *B. M.* diſtil off the Vinegar; until in the Bottom remain a Yellow Powder, inclining to Redneſs. Upon this Powder pour diſtilled Rain-water often times, and as often diſtil it off again, ſtill pouring on freſh diſtilled Rain-water. Repeat this labour ſo long, as until the Powder remain Sweet and * grateful.

*   Our moſt ſincere Author here deceives you not, but conceals a certain Manual Operation, which if you attend to me clearly diſcovering the ſame, the Work it ſelf will never fail to Anſwer your deſire. If you have much Tincture, you muſt have a great Cucurbit; if Little, a leſs will ſerve. For if you take a greater Veſſel, than your Tincture requires, the Vinegar muſt neceſſarily have a greater Fire to cauſe it to aſcend, by reaſon of the height it muſt unavoidably riſe, or it cannot be diſtilled ; and in ſuſtaining ſo forcible a Fire, there is great danger of Corrupting the Tincture it ſelf. Here alſo is required another Caution ; viz. this, after two thirds are diſtilled off, you muſt change your Veſſel, and put the remaining Matter into a leſs Glaſs Body, and thence diſtill off the Vinegar, until the Remanency acquire the juſt thickneſs of a Poultis. Alſo take heed, as Baſilius ſeems to intimate, that you diſtil not off the Vinegar, unto dryneſs, leſt the Tincture by Aduſtion be wholly corrupted.*

*   Notwithſtanding all This my own Precaution now given, I could not chooſe, but labour a whole year to little purpoſe, often repeating this Tincture with a vain endeavour, whence I was almoſt as often weary of Chymiſtry through deſperation; for my Tincture was of no efficacy in Medicine; becauſe a meer Caput-mortuum only, unſavoury and of no value. Hence conſider, how little any Proceſs profits, whether ſet down in Writing, or received from a Friend by word of mouth, unleſs you ſet to your hand, and practically learn every particular of the Work fit to be obſerved in operating. Alſo ſee, how liberally I deal with you, in revealing that, the ignorance of which hath put me to great trouble and charge. The manual Operation, which is requiſite for edulcorating*

*this Pap-like Matter remaining in the bottom, is this. upon this Matter pour
diſtilled water, and gently abſtract the ſame by Balneo. when you have repeated this a third time, you will find the water to come off ſweet ; which time
muſt be obſerved with very great diligence. For if you be deceived in that,
your work is at an end, all your labour loſt , and you ſhall get nothing , but a
Caput Mortuum. For as ſoon as twenty, or at moſt thirty drops of ſweet
water come forth , an Acidity appears again and diſtils forth, which the un-
wary judging to be an Acidity of the Vinegar formerly added, proceed in diſtilling , expecting the water to come forth ſweet ; but this being the Acidity
of Antimony, which (the Vinegar being extracted) immediatly follows the
Sweet water, that perſiſting to diſtil deſtroys the whole Virtue of the Antimony, and leaves nothing remaining but an unſavoury Caput-mortuum. Therefore be thou more wary, and as ſoon as this Sweet water comes forth, ceaſe to diſtil, and take out the Pap-like Matter reſiding in the Bottom, and putting that
into another Glaſs, permit it to dry at the Solar-Heat; or elſe evaporate all its
moyſture with moſt gentle Fire, that it may remain a dry Powder: and when
you have avoyded this danger, then go on.*

‘ This Powder grind upon a Marble or Glaſs, firſt
made hot ; then put it in a Glaſs Body, and pour
upon it of the beſt rectified *Spirit* of *Wine*, ſo much
as will ſtand above it three Fingers thickneſs : then
ſet it in a Digeſtive heat, as above , for extracting
the *Tincture* of *Antimony*, which will be high coloured and pleaſantly red to amazement; and it will
depoſit a certain Earth , or feculency in the bottom.

‘ This *Extraction* is ſweet, grateful, and ſo very
efficacious in *Medicine*, as no man, that hath not experienced the ſame , will give credit thereunto.
The *Feces* in the bottom retain the Venenoſity, but
the *Extraction* Medicine only, which Experience
hath taught to be a profitable *Remedy* for men and
Beaſts.   For if three or four Granes of this Medicine be taken, it expels the *Leproſie* and *Gallick
Lues* , purifies the *Blood*, drives away *Melancholy*,
and reſiſts all Venom : and whoſoever labours with
Shortneſs of *Breath*, Difficulty of Breathing , or
Prickings of the Sides, he may be cured by the
Uſe of this Medicine: * which effects many other
wonderful

wonderful Things, if rightly adminiſtred, and in
due time.

* *Theſe Medicaments, which perform their Operations, not by ſenſible force,
as* Catharticks, Emeticks, Diaphoreticks, *and the like are wont to operate,
but inſenſibly uniting their own more pure Univerſal Spirit unto our Spirits, a-
mend Nature and reſtore it to health, are not to be uſed, unleſs where the Body
hath firſt been cleanſed from the impurities af peccant* Humours, *otherwiſe you
caſt theſe* Pearls *into a Dunghil, where (overwhelmed with Filths) they cannot
ſhine and manifeſt their Virtues. For although, by reaſon of their manifold
Virtues, they may be called* Univerſals, *yet they are to be numbred with* To-
picks, *before which Generals are to be uſed, according to the Opinion of* Ga-
len, *and all Phyſitians.*

The Tincture *here ſpoken of, performs all thoſe* Cures, *which* Baſilius *mentions,
if the uſe of it be continued for ſome time. For where that Saying is of
force,* Medicines uſed help, *continued heal, it muſt certainly be applied to
thoſe eſpecially, which inſenſibly operate.*

That Yellow Powder, of which mention is made
above before it is extracted with Spirit of Wine,
may be ground upon a hot Stone, and then put into
Eggs * boyled hard, in place of the Yolk, which is
to be taken out: ſet theſe Eggs in a moiſt Place, or
Cellar, and the Powder will reſolve into a yellow
Liquor.

* *Indeed ſoft Eggs, according to the Saying, are always warily and ſoftly
to be handled ; but in theſe hard Eggs alſo, I have ſomewhat to adviſe you of ;
for if after you have taken out the Yolk, you be not mindful to break that
Pellicle, which divides it from the White, you will wonder to ſee how your
Balſom will intrude it ſelf within the White, and deprive you of a great part
thereof.*

This admirable *Liquor* heals all green *Wounds*, if
ſoon after a Wound is made, it be put therein with
a ſoft Feather, and the Wound well covered with
a Styptick, or other Preſervative Playſter. All
freſh Wounds inflicted either by Prick or Cut, are
healed by this Liquor, without Putrefaction, Inflammation, or any ſuperfluity of Filth, ſo perfectly; as unto Him, who created Heaven and Earth,

and

and in them inſited ſuch a Medicine, due Thanks
and Prayſe deſervedly ought to be given. In all
old, malignant and corroſive Wounds, uſe this *Ex-*
traction or *Balſom* of *Antimony* , and it will never
fail Thee in thy neceſſity. And thou thy ſelf, after me wilt write an *Encomium* of its Prayſes and
publiſh the Virtues thereof, by which externally
applied miſerable Mortals may be made happy :
for the Wolf and * Cancer yeild to it; Rotten-
neſs in the Bones, malignant Ulcers corroded and
perforate with Worms fly from it, and it reſtores
to priſtine Health, and provides Entertainment for
that with it ſelf, when its fixedneſs ſhall be duly
uſed inwardly, and other Convenient Means duly
applied outwardly.

* *If* Chirurgions *would have give credit to our Author, with how great*
care would they prepare this Balſom *for themſelves, and with how great*
Fruit, and how frequently might they uſe the ſame? For I interpoſing my Judg-
ment muſt ſay, that Baſilius *here comes far ſhort, in expreſſing its due Prayſes ;*
for it performs more, than he declares of it. One ſhort Hiſtory, *drawn from*
the Centuries of my Medicinal Obſervations, will confirm the truth of what I
I have ſaid. A certain Woman, about forty Years of Age, for ſeven
years together ſuffered great dolours in her left Breaſt, which were accompani-
ed with a Tumor and Hardneſs. Thoſe Chirurgeons *and* Phyſicians, *whom*
ſhe adviſed with, did all with one Conſent judge her Diſeaſe to be a Cancer ;
and ſhe was alſo judged to labour with a Cancer, by the Cenſure of that famous
Practitioner, who at Orſcotus *(a Village about the Dukes-Wood) very laudably*
and happily practiſed Chirurgy, and drew to himſelf a vaſt number of People :
for after he had, for three Moneth together, in vain endeavoured to heal this
Diſeaſe, he ſeverely pronounced her Breaſt was to be cut off, or the Diſeaſe
could not be extirpated. The Woman, *reſolving rather to ſuffer all Dolours of*
the Diſeaſe, then to ſuſtain ſo cruel and inhumane a Remedy, came to me. I,
beholding her Breaſt, found it wholly inflamed, and twice as bigg as the other,
and an abundance of thin Humors flowing to the Wound. I purpoſed to try all
I could do, rather than ſuffer this miſerable Woman to periſh; and thinking of
this Balſom reſolved to try, whether That, which in other Diſeaſes had fulfilled
the promiſes of its Author, *would fail me here. Therefore, to the Diſeaſed*
Woman waiting my Anſwer, I ſaid; in eight days time I would reſolve her,
whether there was any hopes of Cure or no, without Cutting off; and there-

upon gave her this Remedy to anoint her Breaſt therewith : and which is very ſtrange , in the Space of two Days the Matter came to Ripeneſs , and a juſt Conſiſtency. Therefore , I then filled with good hope , adjoyned inward and outward Remedies , which ſeemed convenient for the purpoſe , and in two Moneths Space the Womans Breaſt was perfectly healed. Upon this I, not without a peculiar Joy, bleſſed and prayſed the Lord, that had conferred ſo great virtue on this Balſom.

Alſo Glaſs of *Antimony* is by me two ways reduced to an Oyl , in diſtillation (as they call it) by Alembeck.

Take Glaſs of *Antimony* ; as it is made of the *Minera* of *Antimony* , ſubtily pulverized , and extract its Tincture with diſtilled Vinegar ; afterward abſtract the Vinegar thence , and edulcorate the remaining Powder. Then pour on Spirit of Wine, with which extract the Tincture, and circulate it in a Pelican well cloſed, for an intire Moneth. Afterward , diſtil it *per ſe*, without any Addition, with a certain ſingular * Dexterity ; and you will thence receive a wonderful grateful and ſweet Medicine, in the form of a Red Oyl, of which afterward may be formed the Stone of Fire.

* *This is the Work, this the Labour, very few true Sons of Art (whom A-pollo loves) could extract this Tincture by Alembeck. There is need (as Ba-ſilius ſaith) of a cereain peculiar manual Operation. This Tincture I ſought many years , and at length (G O D favouring me) found the ſame. Wilt thou have me diſcover it to Thee by an Ænigma ? I ſee thou deſireſt I ſhould, therefore take this Myſtery, thus.* Alciatus, *painting a Dolphin wreathed about an Anchor, writ theſe Words :* Make not too much haſt. *Eſteem of this Admonition, not only in all your Life, but alſo in this very matter, as very pro-fitable to you : for the haſty Birch (as the ſaying is) brings forth blind Whelps. Therefore I again and again admoniſh you, to cauſe Things to be pre-pared for your Matter, by* Juno, Bacchus *and* Vulcan ; *but, as you love your Life, permit it not ſuddenly to flie, rather deliver it to* Mercury *to be inſtructed by him gradually to accuſtom it ſelf to flying ; yea, bind it with a Cord, leſt (as a Bird got out of a Cage, and paſt your Reach) it through Ignorance ap-proach too near the Sun, and with* Icarus, *having its Feathers burnt, fall head-long into the Sea. But after you have detained it for its due time, looſe its Bonds, that it may fly, and come to thoſe fortunate* Iſlands, *unto which all Sons*

This

of Art direct their Sight, and whereunto all Adeptiſts aim to arrive, as unto their deſired and long ſought Harbour. Here, O Lover of Art, you ſhould not be offended, or angry with me, as if I deluded you (deſirous of the Knowledge of this Secret) by a Tantalick *Apple ſhown. what ſhould I do? I in this Caſe give you advice. would you have me caſt* Pearls *before Swine? and unto all men expoſe the Myſtery, which the Antient kept ſo holily, and might not reveal it, unleſs to the worthy Sons of Art only? Thou thy ſelf wouldeſt bewail nothing more, and wouldeſt even execrate me, for doing ſo. They, who underſtand me, underſtand Art: and unto ſuch as are* Chymiſts, *have I opened the way, which if they diligently travel in, they may arrive, where they deſire to be. No man did ever ſo clearly reveal this to me; but by reading the writings of* Authors, *ſtrenuouſly labouring, and truſting in* GOD *without fainting or deſperation (which is a moſt efficatious kind of Prayer) I at length attained to what I have. Do thou ſtudy, and be diligent, that thou mayeſt comprehend: for he, who, knows how to render* Tinctures *volatile, is already admitted into the very Penetrale and Conclave of the Chymical Art; becauſe of all other Myſteries the Method is the ſame. Peruſe the Fables, ſearch into the Riddles, and conſider the Parables of all wiſe men; they all tend hither, and all ſay the ſame. Compare the Parables of others, with this my* Ænigma, *and this with them, that you may underſtand how much Light I have added in all, and how Eaſie I have made the way to thoſe ſerene Temples of Wiſdom.*

This Oyl is the *Quinteſcence*, and the higheſt, that can be written of *Antimony*; as you may find in my former Writings, wherein I have made a ſhort Declaration of *Antimony*, and in which I ſhewed alſo, that there are four *Inſtruments* required for its *Preparation*, and the fifth is that, in which *Vulcan* hath fixed his Reſidence. Underſtand thus: four *Preparations* muſt be made before it can be perfected; and the fifth is the Utility, and effect of the Work in the Body of man. The firſt Labour is *Calcination* and *Liquefaction* into Glaſs. The ſecond is *Digeſtion*, by which *Extraction* is performed. The third is *Coagulation*. The fourth is *Diſtillation* into Oyl, and after that Separation follows *Fixation*, by the ultimate *Coagulation*, through which the Matter is deduced to a perlucid *Fiery Stone*: which that it may operate upon Metals, muſt be fermented, for acquiring its penetrative Property; but

but not fo much, as that Ancient Stone of Philofophers, becaufe it is not Univerfal, but only tingeth particularly. Touching which, about the
End of this Book, more fhall be fpoken when we
treat of the Stone of Fire.

This diftilled Oyl * of which we have now fpoken, effects all things, that are neceffary to be known
by a *Phyfician*, and which he hath need of, in his
Cures.

* Had I not known Bafilius, I fhould have thought him, in this place to
have dealt like a Deceiver, or Vagabond Medicafter with you : but the Matter
it felf unto me, fo often fpeaks for him, as I religioufly fcruple even in the
leaft to doubt his Promifes. For whatfoever I have experienced (but there are
very few Proceffes contained in this Book, which I have not tryed : for He,
from the very firft, was my Teacher, Friend and Patron) I have found fo
very efficacious beyond the Author's Promifes, that it feems to me, he hath been
fparing in declaring the virtues of his Medicaments, leaft in prayfing them,
he fhould be thought too much to commend himfelf. Yet I fhall not here in
his ftead, undertake to comment much on their laudable Virtues. Let him who
believes not, make tryal, that he may know. Whofoever fhall by his own incre-
dulity be deterred from experiencing the Truth hereof, he will fuffer punifhment
enough for his Offence, by the want of the fruit of the fame. For this Oyl, if
rightly ufed in its time, is a Medicine truly univerfal. Confider, I pray, what
I fay, if rightly ufed in its time, that is, the Body being firft purged from grofs
and crude Humours, and general Medicines ufed (as you may remember I did
before admonifh) this Oyl is an univerfal Medicine, for healing all Difeafes Cu-
rable. For Chymifts are not fo mad, or conceited, by reafon of the Goodnefs and
Virtue of their Medicaments, as not to judge fome Difeafes to be unfanable.
Who can reftore any of the Principal Members abfumed by putridnefs? yet I
would not have all Difeafes judged unfanable, by thefe our Chymical Remedies,
which are every where vulgarly condemned as fuch. As for Example, how often have I reftored the Cryftalline Humour taken away; which who judgeth
not impoffible to be reduced? But, of thefe and the like, another place will be more
fit to write. Only of this Medicament I fay, that it heals Feavers of every
kind; yea, even the Quartan it felf (that ancient Reproach of Phyficians)
and in Chronical Diftempers manifefts wonderful Effects: Here among many of
my Obfervations I will give you one only Experiment. In the Year 1655. A
young Maid, aged twenty one Years, fwollen to an enormous Grofsnefs with the
Dropfie, came to me for help. I took this only for her Medicine. For I gave
her no other thing, then this very Medicament twice a Day, to which I dayly
added a Clifter: and in twenty dayes fhe had fweat fo much, as her Body was

The

leſſned half an Ell. Within that Space of twenty Days, as I ſaid, ſhe alſo voyded of urine (provoked by the ſame Medicament) not a little, but her Sweat was wonderful.

Note: *my Friend, and Lover of Art, that this Oyl, whether you prepare it your ſelf, or receive it from another prepared by him, doth not imitate other Diaphoreticks in operating, which being uſed, will in their firſt Doſe provoke Sweats. For if this be given to a Patient whoſe Body is obſtructed with Humors, the firſt Doſe acts nothing, but gently opens the Paſſages, that Sweats may be procured; the next day it cauſeth a gentle and kindly breathing of Sweats only; the third Day it Sweats moderately; but the fourth Day, and thence forward, it cauſeth ſuch an abundance of Sweat, as the Waters proceeding thence run through the Bed upon the Floor. Here is need of a true Phyſician; Hercules Club will profit little, if not in the Hand of Hercules himſelf.*

The Doſe of it before Coagulation is eight Grains taken in Wine. It makes a man very young again, delivers him from all Melancholy, and whatſoever in the Body of man grows and increaſeth, as the Hairs and Nayls, falls off, and the whole man is renewed as a *Phœnix* (if ſuch a feigned Bird, which is only here for Example ſake named by me, can any where be found upon the Earth) is renewed by Fire. And this Medicine can no more be burned by the Fire, than the Feathers of that unknown *Salamander:* for it conſumes all Symptoms in the Body, like conſuming Fire, to which it is deſervedly likened; it drives away every Evil, and expels all That, which *Aurum-Potabile* is capable to expel. The * *Aſtrum* of *Sol* only excels every Medicine of the World when rightly prepared to perfect Fixation: for the *Aſtrum* of *Sol*, and the *Aſtrum* of *Mercury* ariſe almoſt from the very ſame Blood of their Mother, and from one Original of vivifick Sanity.

---

* *Let no man here prodigally or raſhly waſt his own Gold, now he hears of the Aſtrum of Sol, nor expoſe himſelf to ſo great Hazard, as to enter a perillous Combat with vulgar Mercury. In the Chymical World another Sol ſhines, and another Mercury attends on Jupiter. Yet the Chymical Sol, or Mercury here, is not Gold, but more excellent than all Gold; yea, more potent than every*

Now

Mercury, *although fabulous, and feigned to be capable to restore the Dead to Life: it is the Gold, and Argent-vive of Philosophers, which* Basilius *here hints at. But we have treated, and must treat of* Antimony *only.*

Now, no man hath cause to fear, that this Oyl of *Antimony* Extracted first with distilled Vinegar, and afterward with most pure and subtle Spirit of Wine, and then further exalted (as highly as possible) by *Vulcan*, will in any wise purge, or excite frequent Stools, or make any Alterations: for it effects nothing of all this, but by Sweat, Urine, and Spittle, expels the very Root of the Disease to amazement, and restores whatsoever is corrupted by any Symptom.

But Common Glass of *Antimony*, being ground to Powder, put into a little Wine (*viz.* six Grains or more of the Glass, according to the strength of Nature) and that mixture set in heat for one Night, and in the Morning the Wine * poured off clear from the remaining Powder, and so drunk by the Patient, purgeth downward exciting several Stools, and oftentimes also provokes Vomiting, by reason of the Mercurial immature Property, which is yet inherent in the Glass, as every intelligent Physician will easily judge, and indeed he ought further to Examine how this Glass, when he would purge with it, ought to be proved, and administred in a due Dose.

---

* *This is a Common* Vomitory, or Emetick Wine, *well known, which all wandering* Empiricks *now use in all Places, sometimes with a prosperous, sometimes the Contrary, always ambiguous Success; which proceeds partly from the Physician, and partly from the Medicine. This is a Thing to be bewayled; for as histories relate, that* George Castriot *King of the* Epirots, *when the Emperour of the Turks had often asked him, how his Sword, which he had sent, when Peace was made, according to his agreement with the Turk, could perpetrate such wonders as he spake of, saying he saw not any thing singular in it, made this Answer: I did indeed send the Sword of* Scanderbeg *but not* Scanderbeg's *Arm, with which that Sword was managed, so as to perform so great*

Miracles: *fo* , *very many Chymical Medicines, are either dead, or (which is more to be deplored) oftentimes the Caufes of Death , when not managed by the hand of a skilful Doctor. Which unhappy Succefs of this Medicine is caufed from the Mercurial Properties, with which it is too much impregnated (as Ba-filius well notes in this Place) and which I am wont to correct in this manner.*

Take Glafs of Antimony , *moft pure,* ℥iiij. Venetian Borax ℥ß. *melt them together. This being artificially done, you will have a Green Glafs tranf-parent as an* Emrald. *Grind this to a fubtle Power, upon which pour French-Wine, and permit the mixture to ftand for feveral days in a Moderate Heat.*

Of this Wine give to the Sick , from ℈j. *to* ℥ij, *according to the Age, Habit of Body, Strength, and other Things either Natural, or not Natural, which the Prudence of the Phyfician (when he fits as Judge, whether the Life of any One is likely to be continued or not) ought always well to confider. That this* Emetick Wine *may be given to the Sick without peril , Experience the moft certain Miftrefs of* Phyficians *hath taught me , and yet more than this : for when the Wine poured in the Powder fhall be all exhaufted, if you pour on more French Wine, that will alfo be imbibed with the fame Virtues. For here* Antimony *difcovers in it felf to be fomewhat, that is of all wonderful Things the moft admirable : becaufe it contains in it felf inexhauftible Treafures, and although you take from it , yet you diminifh not the Virtues thereof. A like ftupendious Miracle alfo is in extracting the Vinegar of the fame, and in other Works fit to be kept under the Seal of* Harpocrates.

Many men are required for the Searching out the Powers and Virtues of this Subject. For I a-lone, by reafon of the fhortnefs of my Time , could not dive into and fearch out all things, do thou thy felf fet about the Work , and after me , yea with me, thou wilt praife me and I thee : if you find out any more ; I praife you by thefe my Writings, and fhall commend you out of the Sepulcher to which I am deftinated, although in Body thou art to me unknown , nor ever had I any difcourfe with thee, becaufe perhaps not yet born.

Common Glafs of *Antimony* is alfo by Addition diftilled into a laudable and falutary oyl, which may be ufed without peril, with very great profit in the *Epilepfie* ; as here following I fhall teach.

Grind the Glafs of *Antimony* to as fubtle a Pow-der as poffibly you can, then put it into a Glafs-Veffel with a flat Bottom, and pour upon the Pow-der

der the *Juice* of *unripe Grapes*, then having well
luted the Veſſel digeſt it for certain Days. This
being done abſtract all the Juice; afterward, grind
it well moyſtned with Spirit of Vinegar, and a
double Weight of clarified Sugar. Then, having
put it into a Retort, in the Name of the Moſt High
begin to diſtil, and at laſt adminiſter a vehement
Fire, and you will acquire a moſt Red Oyl; which
muſt be clarified unto Tranſparency with * Spirit
of Wine.

* *When the* Author *ſaith, it muſt be clarified with* Spirit of Wine *unto*
Tranſparency; the Admonition is ſhort indeed, but of great weight. For he
wills, that this Oyl ſhould be driven over by Alembeck; the ſignification and
manual Operation of which, I have already above taught.

The Uſe of this, given in a ſmall Quantity, is
found to be moſt profitable. With this Oyl Spirit
of Salt may be joyned, and the Mixture poured upon a ſubtle prepared Calx of Gold, (which how it
ſhould be made I have already taught in other of
my Writings) which hath before, together with its
Water, paſſed by Alembeck. If this be done, this
Menſtruum takes to its ſelf the Tincture * of Gold
only, and leaves the Body untouched.

* *Do you think, O Lover of Chymiſtry, you underſtand what you read ?*
You cannot underſtand, unleß either divinely Philip, *or humanely* Oedipus,
appear to you, and clearly teach you the way of preparing this Tincture. The
difficulty of the Ænigma conſiſts in this; viz. that all Menſtruums, with
which Tinctures are extracted, muſt neceſſarily be void of Colour; otherwiſe
how can you know: whether you obtain the Tincture you would extract, or on-
ly retract the ſame you poured on ? I will not detain you with a tedious Diſ-
courſe full of ambiguities, but lead you as it were by the hand, ſhewing you
how I inſtituted this Proceß in the Year 1665. *If you thence, by your attenti-*
on, and comparing the precedent with the preſent, and theſe with thoſe that
follow, reap any profit, open the Boſom of your Heart, that no part of this may
fall to the Earth.
I took that Red Oyl, thus far prepared as is already ſhewed, and rectified it
by Retort; *and then acquired a White Oyl, of an acid but grateful Taſte.*

upon this I *powred half fo much* Spirit of Salt : *the Mixture* I *digefted in a Phial for a full Month , that thefe two Spirits might be well conjoyned ; afterward , for the better conjunction of them ,* I *diftilled them thrice by* Retort. *Then* I *poured them upon the Calx of Gold (the Method of preparing which you will find in other writings of* Bafilius*) and fet them together in Digeftion for a Month ; which being elapfed , the* Menftruum *was tinged with a deep Yellow Colour inclining to rednefs.* I *leifurely poured off the Tincture , and having put it into a* Retort *, with gentle Fire abftracted the Humidity , that a red Pouder might remain in the Bottom. This Powder* I *edulcorated with diftilled water , and again extracted the Tincture with Spirit of wine; then* I *rendred this* Dragon *volatile , and gave him his own Tayl to be devoured for fix whole Months , and obtained a Tincture moft pleafant and grateful ; ten or twelve Grains of which given to the Sick, provoke Sweat, comfort the Natural Powers , and (not to amufe the Intelligent with words) in all Difeafes both of Humane and other Bodies, it is an univerfal Medicine.*

Since it hath happened to me here to make mention of the moft excellent of all Tinctures, I *will once teach the Chymift what will be of ufe to him for the future. That is to fay , it is of great concern to know , with what* Menftruum *every Tincture fhould be extracted, For it is not fufficient (according to the erroneous Opinion of many) that* Menftruums *be fweet and void of* Corofion; *but it is alfo behooful , that there be in them a peculiar Amity and Conveniency with the* Mercury *of the Body, on which they are poured, that from the fame they may extract its true and fincere Sulphur. By Example,* I *fhall teach you fomewhat more clearly. Diftilled water extracts the Tincture from Sulphur, made of the Glafs of* Antimony *by diftilled Vinegar. But if in this Operation you perfwade your felf you have feparated the Pure from the Impure, you will be deceived : for this water imbibes a certain* Salt, *which infects the Tincture; but Spirit of wine rectified is its proper* Menftruum: *becaufe That only affumes the volatile Sulphur thereof, and hath no Commerce with the* Salt.

The fame happens in Tincture of Corals , which is extracted with Spirit of wine diftilled upon Orange Pills : for here you obtain not the fincere Tincture of Corals; becaufe, by this Menftruum, *the pure Sulphur is not feparated from the Body of the Corals. The like Error to be committed in many other Things,* I *have obferved by Experience, which fhould be efteemed the beft Miftrefs, unlefs we take it for granted that chargeable and fruitlefs Proceffes are neceffarily required in this Art. But that* I *may conclude with the Tincture, whence all this Difcourfe hath proceeded;* I *would have no man to think this to be the* Aurum potabile *of Philofophers : for this would be a very great Error in Philofophy, and give occafion to Sophifters (as their manner is) to prefer their Sophifms before the Truth it felf. Although this Tincture is moft precious, and a Tincture of Gold, yet it hath only affumed the Colour of Gold : but the weight thereof, which is proper to* Aurum potabile, *adheres not thereunto.*

Touching the potable Medicine here is not place of fpeaking , unlefs I *would tranfgrefs the limits, which* I *have at this time prefcribed my felf, of Comment-*

When

ing upon the Triumphant Chariot *of* Antimony *, which our* Eafil Valentine *hath made for it fo truly magnificent. Otherwife, I fhould declare, how* Sol *might be prepared by* Venus *and* Vulcan *, fo as in the fpace of two hours to refolve it felf into* Mercury *united with* Bacchus, *leaving very few feces ; which* Mercurial Menftruum *may again be feparated from the refolved* Gold*; and fo you might acquire a moft grateful Liquor very ponderous, which can never afterward be reduced to its former Confiftence. This very Operation I have fhewed to fome Curious Lovers of* Chymiftry. *But of thefe elfewhere another Occafion of writing will be given.*

When the Fermentation is made, I fhall have need of a vaft Quantity of Paper to declare all the *Arcanum*'s of Nature, which by this Medicine are effected beyond the Opinion of all men. I urge this fo much the more earneftly to the Phyfician, that he may confider thofe things which I propofe Philofophically, betake himfelf to labour, perform this Preparation of *Antimony* , and deduce it to Ufe ; then, he himfelf will dayly find more Praife, and learn from it more Operations than any of the other Phyficians could have prefcribed him.

When you fhall have brought *Antimony* fo far, and duely perfected your Work, in which you are to act prudently, and the matter is to be largely and profoundly weighed, that by Labour you may acquire Experience ; then may you boaft that you have obtained the Magiftery, which is known or communicated to few. This Magiftery mix'd with a Solution or Tincture of Corals, and exhibited with Cordial Water effects Wonders in Difeafes, that are to be cured by purifying the Blood. And whatfoever Diftemper is offered to you, in which the Blood is corrupted by any Accident, this Magiftery heals it , exhilarates the Heart, promotes Chaftity and Honefty , and renders man apt and fit for every thing he takes in hand.

For all thefe Benefits to the *Creator* and *Conferver* of all Things, thanks is always to be given from the bottom of our Heart; becaufe he hath

G   with

with ſo great Compaſſion reſpected his *Creatures*,
Infirm both in Body and Mind, and ſupplied us with
Means , by which the Diſeaſes of either may be
healed , and we in every neceſſity obtain ſolace,
aſſiſtance and perfect Help.

Now my Intention is to proceed , and ſpeak
ſomewhat of the *Arcanum* of *Antimony*, but with
very great Brevity.

Take of *Antimony* moſt ſubtlely pulverized
1. Part, of *Sal-Armoniack* *, ſo called , which is
brought from *Armenia,*

* *Of* Antimony *and* Sal-Armoniack *equal parts are to be taken , which*
Baſilius *ſeems to intend, but I know not how he forgot to mention it.*

alſo pulverized ; mix theſe, and putting them into
a Retort diſtil them together, *

* *That with one and the ſame labour, the* Sal-Armoniack *together with the*
Antimony, *may be diſtilled and ſublimed, ſuch an Inſtrument as this I here*
ſhew you, deſcribing all its Parts, may be made.

Here place the Figure in the 82 Page.

A. *is the Fornace.* B. *the Retort.* C. *the Recipient.* D. *the Aperture with*
a Pipe of a Moderate bigneſs, on which may be ſet the Alembeck E. *The other For-*
nace is F, *which containing a moderate Fire, ſublimes what falls into the re-*
ceiving Veſſel up into the Alembeck E. *And ſo the Matter which is diſtilled*
from the Retort E, *by the Fire of the Fornace* F, *is preſently ſublimed; which*
may not only be uſeful in this Caſe , but alſo in every Sublimation of other
Matters.

and upon that which comes forth in the Diſtillation
pour common diſtilled Rain-water , but let it firſt
be made hot , and ſo by edulcorating remove all.
the *Salt*, that no Acrimony may remain , and the
Antimony will appear like pure, white ſhining Feathers. Dry them with ſubtle Heat , and having
put them in a Glaſs circulatory or Pelican, pour

. on

on them good and perfectly rectified *Spirit* of *Vi-triol*, and Circulate the Mixture till both be well conjoyned * and united, then diftill the whole, and pour on *Spirit* of *Wine*, circulate again; then let feparation be made, and remove the *Feces* fetling to the Bottom, but keep the *Arcanum* which re- mains mixt with the *Spirit* of *Wine* and *Vitriol*.

* *This* Union *muſt be ſo firm, as in diſtilling one may not be ſeparated from the other; otherwiſe you will loſe your Labour and Coſt. Of how great moment this* Union *is in* Chymiſtry, *they beſt know, who only by confounding two things together, think they ſhall effect Wonders; but afterwards (their Experience failing them) they learn how great difference there is between* Union *and* Confuſion : *for Things confounded receive no Virtue, that was not in them before; but by* Union, *I know not what* Spirit *is ingeſted, which performs ſuch things as the Mind of man could never perceive to have their being thence. Hence conſider in the Generation of Animals (who would believe it!) how from the* Union *of Elements is generated Sight, Taſt, Touching, and ſo many Powers of Animals, which are infited in none of the Elements, and yet ariſe from them united. Whenſoever it happens, that any Tincture ſeems to have u- nited it ſelf with its* Menſtruum, *and afterward may be ſeparated therefrom, that therefore is becauſe Matrimony is not legitimately Celebrated, nor the union in a due manner perfect; which you ſhall more than once ſee to happen in the Tincture of* Sol *and* Antimony.

The Inſtrument, *by which I conjoyn my Tinctures, and am wont to copulate them in an undiſſolvible Copulation, you ſhall find deſcribed hereafter in this very Book. That in* Spirit *of* Wine *is to be noted, which happens not in other Menſtruums; becauſe it is moſt eaſily united to Things, and again with a ſlight artifice ſeparated from the ſame.*

Now when you again rectifie this *Arcanum*, one drop of it exhibited with Roſe- water, is more a- vailable than a Pot full of the Decoction of Herbs; for it cauſeth a good Appetite, corrects the Sto- mach, and concocts all malignity in it, drives away Sadneſs and Melancholy, makes good Blood and a good Digeſtion; in the Suffocation of the Matrix and Cholick Paſſion (both which it wonderfully appeaſeth) it is inſtead of a Treaſure of ineſtima- ble price, and deſerves Commendation, not eaſily expreſſible by Words,

After the *Arcanum* of *Antimony* next in order follows the *Elixir* * of the same, which you may prepare in this manner.

Take, in the name of the Lord, good *Minera* of *Antimony*, grind it subtlely, and sublime it with half so much *Sal-Armoniack*. Whatsoever shall be sublimed put into a Glass Retort, and thrice distil it, separating the *Feces* every time. Afterward remove from it the *Sal-Armoniack* by edulcoration, and reverberate the Matter of *Antimony* in a Vessel well closed, with moderate Fire (not forcing too much) until it become like the Earth of *Cinnabar*. This being done, pour on it strong distilled Wine Vinegar, and extract its Redness; afterward abstract the Vinegar, until a Powder remain. This Abstraction must be made in *Balneo*. Then, extract this Powder with Spirit of Wine, that the *Feces* may be separated, and you will have a pure and clear Extraction. Having finished this Operation, put this Spirit of Wine together with the Extraction into a *Cucurbit*, and add thereto a little of the Tincture of Corals, and of the Quintessence of Rubarb, and then administer the Dose of three or four Grains.

It causeth gentle Stools, and purgeth without Gripings of the Belly ; and indeed if you have proceeded well in preparing, it renders the Blood agil', and is a Medicine apt for those who desire Gentle Purgations.

Here perhaps some *Physician* may wonder, how 'tis possible, that this Medicine should cause moderate and easie Purgations, when as *Antimony* is a

Matter

Matter vehement and forcible, and to it is joyned
Rubarb, which of it self alfo hath a Purging Property. But let him ceafe his admiration, and know
that the venomous purging power of *Antimony* is
by this Preparation fo mortified, as it can apprehend or expel nothing ; but as foon as fome purging Simple is adjoyned to it, it then according to
the powers of its own Nature performs the Office
of opening and purging. But *Antimony* prepared
hath no action upon the * Stomach, thence to expel its impurities; but by the purging Medicine,
its adjunct, acquires a more open Field, and therein
can operate without Impediment any other way,
and difcern , yea fearch ont the way of Effecting
that better,to which it was ordained and prepared,
without hindrance.

Note here very ferioufly , that Galenick Catharticks *have power of expelling, but not of Correcting Humors ; but Chymical Purgers are endued with either Faculty; and certainly it fhould not be minded how much is expelled, but
how much is healed, which the occult power of Medicaments prepared Chymically doth much better effect, than that common and publick violence of purging
forcibly.*

    I would have all men to credit thefe my words,
fince I have no neceffity to write other than the
Truth. This *Elixir* in fuch manner prepared, as I
have taught, penetrates and purgeth the Body, as
Antimony purgeth Gold, and frees it from all Impurity: So that if I would at large commemorate all
the powers and virtues thereof, I muft put up my
Supplications to the *G O D* of Heaven , and in-
treat him to vouchfafe me a longer Life, that I
might laud his wonderful Works, and fearch out
further , and according to Verity communicate to
others what I have found, that they with me excited
to admiration , may publickly render thanks to
their *Creator*, for his fo great Bleffings.

But to proceed in my purpoſe, having once begun, I here deſcribe the Virtues of *Antimony*, as far
as I have experienced them; yet what is hid from
my knowledge, I ought to paſs over in ſilence.
For it becomes me not to give my Judgment of
things unknown, and which I have not my ſelf ex-
perimented, but I leave them, commending the ſame
to other Judges, who with ſtudy and labour in this
Subject, have made ſome good progreſs. No one
man can be ſo expert in knowing the Virtues of
Antimony, as nothing ſhall remain unknown by him,
not only by reaſon of the ſhortneſs of his Life (as I
before ſaid) but alſo, and chiefly becauſe ſome new
thing is dayly found in it.

Therefore, let men know, that *Antimony* not on-
le purgeth Gold, cleanſeth and frees it from every
peregrine Matter, and from all other Metals, but
alſo (by a power innate in it ſelf) effects the ſame in
Men and Beaſts. If a Farmer purpoſe in himſelf
to keep up and fatten any of his Cattle, as for
Example an Hog; two or three days before, let
him give to the Swine a convenient Doſe of crude
Antimony, about half a dram mix'd with his Food,
that by it he may be purged; through which Pur-
gation he will not only acquire an Appetite to his
Meat, but the ſooner increaſe and be fatned. And
if any Swine labour with a Diſeaſe about his Liver
or other Parts, or elſe be Leprous, *Antimony* cauſeth
the Leproſie to be dryed up and expelled.

This Example ſeems indeed to ſound ſomewhat
groſs and ruſtical, to the Ears of Great men eſpecially; but my purpoſe in propoſing it only was to
the end, that private Men and *Laicks*, whoſe Brains
were not by Nature fabricated to the moſt ſubtle
Philoſophy of the Learned, may ſee the Truth hereof, in the very Operation it ſelf, with their own
Eyes; alſo that by this rude Propoſal, they might
give

give greater credit to my other Writings, in which
I have spoken a little more subtely of these Things.
Yet I would have no man, following me as his Author, to give a Medicine of Crude *Antimony* to
men; for mute Animals can in their Stomach concoct much more hard Foods, than the tender Complexion of Men is able to digest. Wherefore, he
who would rightly and with profit use *Antimony*,
he must learn the Preparation thereof first, and afterward know the Dose, as what is convenient for
the Young, and what for the Old; how much may
be given to robust Bodies, and how much to the
weak, in which no small Mystery of this Art consists,
the ignorance of which will do more hurt than an
imprudent Physician can do good.

Should I confirm all things by Examples, that
would be the Cause of a very Prolix Writing;
therefore I will break off this Discourse, and pass
on to another Preparation of *Antimony*, and describe its fixedness; which acts like Wine, from
which its Spirit is substracted and separated from
its Body. This Spirit heals the Body internally,
and if externally applied, draws to it self all the Heat
of a part inflamed : but, on the contrary, when
of the Wine, Vinegar is made, it cools, either inwardly or outwardly applied; although the Wine
and Vinegar have their Original from the same
Root, and proceed from the same Stock. The
Reason of this diversity is, because Vinegar is
made through digestion only, by which Putrefaction of the Wine follows, together with a Vegetable Fixation: but on the contrary, Spirit of Wine
is made with Separation by distilling, or vegetable
subliming, which renders the Spirit volatile. By
like reason *Antimony* is prepared, and according
to its divers Preparations hath divers Effects, and
diversly communicates its Gifts to us, which are

G 4   scarcely

fcarcely comprehenfible by the humane Intellect. But the Fixedness thereof, touching which I here treat, is thus prepared.

Take of *Antimony* as much as you will, grind it to a fubtle Powder, which put into a *Cucurbit*, and pour on it of *Aqua fortis* fo much as will ftand above it the breadth of fix Fingers; and having well and firmly clofed the Veffel, place it in a fubtle heat for ten Days, that the Matter may be extracted. Decant off this Extraction pure and clear, and filter it, that it may be free from all feculencies and Impurities; then put this Extraction into a Glafs-Body, and abftract all the *Aqua fortis* by Diftillation in Afhes or Sand, and in the bottom the Powder of *Antimony* will remain yellow and dry. Upon this pour diftilled Rain-water, and put it in a like Glafs in moderate heat, and you will have a Red Extraction. This again filter, and gently diftil off the Rain-water by *B. M.* and the Powder will remain red in the Bottom. Upon this red Powder pour ftrong diftilled Vinegar: this Vinegar will in fome time draw to it felf the Colour red as Blood, and put down *Feces*. Afterward diftil off the Vinegar, and there will again remain a red Powder. This Powder reverberate continually for three days together without ceafing in an open Fire; This being done, abftract the Tincture from it by Spirit of Wine, and feparate the *Feces* remaining from the Tincture. All thefe Works being with fo great labour performed, again feparate the Spirit of Wine by diftillation in *Balneo*, and a fixed * Red Powder will remain, which operates wonderfully.

---

* Diaphoretick Antimony *is fold in Shops, but what here the Author fhews us, by the name of Fixed Powder of Antimony, is not to be bought for filver or Gold; the Virtues of which fo far exceed all that, of which the common Sort are Partakers: It vain with fo great attention and ftudy (of*

which in preparing this Powder, there is very great need) did our Philosopher intend this Work, if these Mysteries of so great Effects must come to the handling of the Vulgar, or be publickly sold for Money. Let him who attains to this fixed Powder use it in Chronical Diseases, especially where Sweats are to be excited, and he will see Effects causing him to rejoyce, if he use it in himself; and by which he will be glorified, if he use it in others.

Half a dram of this being taken thrice a day, *viz.* Morning, Noon, and Night, or oftner, hurts no man; for it expels all clotted Blood out of the Body, and being long taken securely opens all perillous Imposthums, and expels them; radically cures the *French Disease*, causeth new Hairs to grow, and notably renovates the whole man.

Now, since I have taught to make a fixed Powder of *Antimony*, and the Extraction thereof very commodious for Use, leaving this Discourse, I purpose briefly to treat of the Flowers of *Antimony*, which may be many ways prepared. But the greatest part * of men neither can discourse of, nor answer to these; because they have not learned the Processes of such Operations: but the least part, *viz.* the Disciples, Apostles, and Followers of the *Spagyrick Art*, will more esteem my Writings, more diligently read them, and more prudently give Judgement of the same.

---

* *How much* Chymistry *was impeached by Calumnies, in the times of* Basilius, *is manifest by the very many Reliques of writers, with which some* Theologicians, *imprudently judging what they understood not, and Politicians (not much more prudent than them) have defamed their own Books; and in the mean while also given occasion to Others, more throughly searching into the matter, of judging those very Authors, with no greater circumspection to have likewise bespattered other innocent Persons with their Censure. I do not here speak of those Writers, who sharply reprehend certain Vagabond Sophisters, that covering their own Wickedness, under the Pretext of a most noble Art, do by a great Name impose great Frauds upon the People. For this kind of men are not only worthy of severe Reprehension, but also of due Punishment. But, what Evil do they deserve, if under their Denomination the Good be abused?*

But,

Why is the moft certain and fo falutary and profitable an Art proferibed ? Becaufe there are men found, which ufe not the Art it felf, but the Name and Shadow of this Art. Yet I am unwilling to prolong this Apology, leſt Envy, which hath been the greateſt Caufe of Calumny, fall upon me in this manner lamenting, whilſt I hear Bafilius encouraging his , and have reaſon to applaud our own Times, in which fome part of that moſt thick Cloud, which caſt out fo many Tounders, is already vaniſhed. In Shops they now fell Medicaments, Chymically prepared (as they fay) and thoſe very Perſons, who are willing moſtly to be eſteemed Hippocratick Difciples , fcarcely dare to condemn Chymiſtry, and fince they call into ufe what are made by the Chymical Art, they cannot deny it. Are not thoſe Times at hand, in which Elias the Artiſt, the Revealer of greater Myſteries is to come ? Of whoſe Coming Paracelfus fo clearly prophefied in various places of his Writings ? Perhaps it will be worth our while, for the Solace of the oppreſſed Difciples of Bafilius, to quote certain places, in which he prediĉts the coming of Elias not then born: which if any One commodiouſly interpret, as all other Sayings of that man are to be taken , he will find nothing of abfurdity in them, unleß he refolve to difcover his own abfurd Stupidity , or wicked Envy. In the Book of Minerals, Chap. 8. Paracelfus thus writes : What is moſt vile, G O D fuffers to be difcovered, but what is of greater moment is yet hid from the Vulgar, until the coming of Elias the Artiſt ; others read , until the Art of Elias , when he comes. And again, in his Book of Minerals, Treatiſe the firſt. It is indeed true (faith he) that many things lie hid in the Earth, which I, as well as others am ignorant of. For this I know, G O D, in time to come will manifeſt his wonders, and bring to light many more of them, then unto this Day have been known by us. Alfo this is true; there is nothing abfconded , which fhall not be revealed ; therefore there cometh One, whoſe Magnale lives not yet , who fhall reveal many Things.

Therefore be comforted, be comforted , O Lover of Chymiſtry , and prepare the way of that Elias, who brings happy times, and will reveal more Secrets than our Anceſtors, by reaſon of Envy, and the Iniquity of their Days durſt difcover. whofoever thou art, converfing in this Art , confer fome fmall matter to this felicity ; and let us give the World that Medicine, which by reaſon of evil Humors predominant, it cannot take all at once, by degrees, that it may gradually recover of its Difeafe, and the Times of Elias come (for Arts alfo, as well as is underſtood of other things, have their Elias, faith Theophraſtus) where it will be lawful for us to fpeak freely of theſe things, and openly to do good to our Neighbours, without perfecution of the Impious. Read, underſtand, and comfort your felf with thefe.

But, my Difciple and Follower, if you will imitate me, my advice is, that you take up your Crofs, at firſt, and fuffer as I have fuffered ; learn to bear Perfecution, as I have already born it, labour, as
all

all our Predeceſſors with me have done; with continual Prayers ſeek unto the Lord *G O D*, and be
thou patient, and laborious without wearineſs, and
then the *Moſt High*, who hath mercifully heard me,
will not forſake Thee: for this Cauſe I every hour
give thanks to *G O D*, as my Eyes filled with Tears
can and do witneſs.

Now, to proceed in my Inſtruction, touching
the *Flowers* of *Antimony*, it is to be underſtood,
that the true *Flores* of *Antimony*, may be prepared,
not one, but various ways, as is known to every
Spagyriſt. There are ſome who drive them, mix'd
with *Sal-Armoniack*, over by Retort; then they
edulcorate them, by waſhing away the *Sal Armoniack*, and theſe they greatly eſteem ; for theſe
Flowers are of a fair and white Colour. Others
have peculiar Inſtruments for this Work, prepared with windy Caverns, through which the *Antimony* may receive the Air, and be ſublimed. O-
thers, ſetting three Alembecks one upon another
ſublime them with ſtrong Fire, and with one and
the ſame labour make white , yellow , and Red
Flores; all which ways I have tried, and found no
Error in them : But the Proceſs, by which I make
Flowers of *Antimony*, moſt profitable for Medicine,
and more efficacious in their Operations is this.

I mixed the red Flowers of *Antimony* with Col-
cothar of Vitriol, and ſublimed them together
thrice. So, the Eſſence of Vitriol aſcends with
them, and the *Flores* are more ſtrong : which being
done, I extract the ſame Flowers with Spirit of
Wine. The *Fæces* ſettle to the bottom, and ſeparate themſelves from the Spirit. Theſe the Artificer lays aſide, and diſtils off the Spirit of Wine
in *B. M.* until the Powder remains dry.

Theſe are my prepared Flowers of *Antimony*,
which I adminiſtred to my Brethren, and others,

who

who in there Neceſſities, required help of me, for
their Souls ſpiritual, in reſpect of my. Ecclefiaftical
State,& for their Bodies temporal,by reaſon of the
Truſt they repoſed in my Art. Theſe *Flores* purge
gently,without frequent,or exceſſive Stools,& have
cured many *Tertian* & *Quartan Fevers*,alſo very many other Diſeaſes;ſo that I purpoſed, by the help of
our Saviour Jeſus,and his moſt Holy Mother *Mary*,
to ordain in my Teſtament a perpetual Monument
upon my Altar,of all the Cures which I have performed by his grace;that I might ſo doing,not only
give thanks to *GOD*, but alſo make my Gratitude
known to Poſterity,that theylikewiſe may acknowledge the wonderful works of the Moſt High,which
I (by my diligence) have extracted from the Bowels
of Nature, and which he himſelf had hid and abſconded in her profound and moſt ſecret Receſſes.

But touching the Sublimations of *Antimony*,which
are afterward called Flowers; let the Reader further obſerve,*viz.* that they are like Waters,which
break out in high Mountains.Now,of the difference
of waters,which ariſe in the higheſt Mountains,yea
in higher than they,if ſuch can be found;for even unto them would the waters aſcend;ſince it is known,
that in the tops of the higheſt Mountains, Springs
do very often iſſue it;and of other waters which are
found by digging deep in the Earth, and by following their Springs muſt be ſearched out:any man may
judge that the *Matrix* of waters in the Earth, is on
one part more aboundantly repleniſhed with the
Riches of waters, then on another;ſince every Element hath a peculiar *Matrix*,either ſtrong or weak,
according as it is produced by the *Sydus*, whence
Elements derive their Original and have being.
Now, when ſuch a *Matrix* is ſtrong and potent in
the Earth, it can drive forth its Seed ſtrongly and
efficaciouſly from it ſelf, by a vehement Preſſure,

even

even up to the Snowy Mountains of the *Alps*, or to
the very top of the *Babylonish* * Tower.

* *This Parable is of very great moment, but so very clear to those, from
whose Eyes the Cataract is taken away, as to explain it to them, would be to
hold a Candle to the Light of the Sun: to others, from whose sight the Cataract
is not took off, this place gives no occasion of detracting the same. Therefore
read, peruse, and meditate; Day is an Instructer to the Day; the later Reading
explains the former, and the former the later.*

If any fatuate man hear this my Difcourfe, he
will fay, I am either mad or drunk with Wine; but
this will be no other than a Reproach, like to that,
which was caft upon the Difciples of our Saviour.
Of Sublimation, the Reafon is the fame; for as
Waters, which are many times found in the higheft
Mountains, are more falubrious, and more cool than
thofe, which by digging deep into the Earth are
found in Plains: fo, if the Matter by prefliure & force
of fire be driven upwards to the Mountains of the
Ancient Wife men, who died long before my time,
the Earth, which for the moft part is unprofitable,
remains until its Salt fhall be extracted from it for
its proper ufe. Thus is made Separation, by which
the Evil may be diftinguifhed from the Good, the
Pure from the Impure, the thick from the thin, the
fubtle from that which is not fubtle, and the Venom
from the Medicament. We miferable Mortals, by
Deathwhich we have deferved for our Sins are put
into the Earth, until we putrefie by time, and be reduced to filths; and afterward by the Heavenly Fire
and Heat raifed, clarified, and exalted to a Celeftial
Sublimation, where all our *Feces*, all Sins, and e-
very Impurity fhall be feparated, and we made the
Sons of *G O D*, and of Eternal Life, unto which
the Lord of his Mercy and Goodnefs bring me
with you. But I hope no Man will take amifs this
Comparation of the Mundane with the Spiritual,
viz. the Heavenly Exaltation with the Earthly Sublimation.

limation. For no man fhould fuppofe what I
have done, to be done without Reafon, but rather
know, that I am ignorant what is white or black,
how much the tenebrous and difmal Air differs
from the ferene and clear Heaven. Therefore let
us break off this Difcourfe, and produce another
Preparation of *Antmony*.

Let the Difciple, Apoftle, and faithful Imitator
of Art, underftand this Inftruction, and according
to the true Philofophick Doctrine faithfully confider, that every Extraction from *Antimony* (as alfo
from all other Things) hath great difference in O-
peration, which neither confifts in the Matter, nor
is known by the Matter, from which it is drawn;
but confifts and remains in the Preparation, and in
the Addition, by which the Virtue is extracted
from the Matter, as is known by Experience; as
for Example. Whatfoever is Extracted from *Antimony*, or any other thing with Spirit of Wine,
hath a far other virtue of Operating, than thofe,
which are extracted with good and fharp Vinegar.
The Caufes of this I have already hinted in my o-
ther Writings; but the principal Caufe is, becaufe all Extractions made with Spirit of Wine,
from *Antimony*, or any purging Herbs, Roots, or
Seeds (underftand of the firft Extraction) powerfully expel by Seidge: but on the contrary, whatfoever is extracted with Vinegar, purgeth not
downward, but rather prevents that, and retains
in a certain peculiar manner, by which the Volatile
is changed into fixed.

This is a fingular Secret, and an *Arcanum* of great
price; but there are none, or very few found, who
mind fuch things; becaufe many things are hidden,
and lie deeply buried in this *Arcanum*, which no
One, either Mafter or Servant, nor any Wife man
of this World hath unto this Day obferved or confidered.   These

Therefore the Extraction of *Antimony* is made two ways, *viz.* with Vinegar, and with Spirit of Wine. Vinegar obstructs, and Spirit of Wine, of it self powerfully expels and causeth Urine, as also Stools ; as elsewhere in another manner is shewed, and especially where I speak of my Twelve Keys, as namely, that the Extraction of Glass of *Antimony* moderately purgeth ; but on the contrary the Extraction of the same Glass, which is made with Vinegar purgeth not: which is true and not permixt with any falsity. But this Experience gives occasion of thinking and reflecting, by which way of Reasoning, Nature gives promotion and production to a true Philosopher. But it is a thing much to be admired, that every Subject, which is first of all extracted with Spirit of Wine, should have a Purging Property. Yet when Glass of *Antimony* is from the beginning extracted with distilled Vinegar, and that Vinegar again abstracted, and then the *Antemony* extracted with Spirit of Wine, all its venomous purging virtue passeth away, and no sign thereof remains, nor assumes it to it self any power of provoking Stools ; but it performs its Operations by Sweat, and other ways, chiefly by Salivation and Ejection by the Mouth ; it searcheth out all hurtful Evils in the Body, purgeth the Blood, heals the Diseases of the Lungs, and profits those who are strait-breasted, and troubled with a frequent Cough. In a word it Cures very many Diseases, also asswageth a Malignant Cough, and whatsoever is of that Disposition, and is a Medicine very admirable.

Moreover, there is another Extraction of *Antimony* made in this manner. Grind crude *Antimony* to powder, and pour upon it strong Vinegar, not of Wine, but made of its proper *Minera*, and expose the Mixture in a Vessel well closed to the

Solar

Solar heat; then, after ſome time the Vinegar will be tinged with a Blood-like Colour, pour off this Extraction clear, filter it, aud diſtil by Alembick in Sand: then again, in diſtilling, it ſhews admirable Colours, pleaſant to the Sight, and wonderful in Aſpect. ·This Oyl * at length becomes Red as Blood, and leaves many *Feces* and prevails againſt many Infirmities: for its ſingular Virtue and Uſe is commanded in the Leproſie ; the New Diſeaſe lately riſen amongſt the Souldiers is by it conſumed and dried up, and indeed it effects Wonders.

* *Here thy Sincerity,* Valentine, *is ſuſpected. Who can by this thyPreſcription make this* Quinteſſence, *which* Petrus *the* Spaniard, *in his Book* Of the Quinteſſenc of all Things, *deſervedly extols, as the greateſt Secret of Philoſophy ? What ſhall I ſay ? Malice makes thee, not a perverſe , but timerous man, fearing, leaſt if* Arcanum's *ſhould be communicated openly to the wicked, they would do more hurt with them then good. This Proceſs ſeems to me to be purpoſely deſcribed obſcurely by this Religious Man (why elſe ſhould he not have written otherwiſe !) becauſe he knew the Sons of Art would underſtand it by his Preſcript. But that you, Reader, may underſtand, you have not in vain ſpent your Money in buying, or time in reading theſe Commentaries, I will clearly and nakedly diſcover to you , how I my ſelf have oftentimes performed this very work : do you give good heed to all Things , that you may not at all be deficient; for the Operations are ſo concatinated , or co-linked together , as one being omitted, or negligently performed, all the other are ſpoyled, and your labour cannot anſwer your Deſires.*

Take of the beſt Minera *of* Antimony, *which is friable (for if you take crude* Antimony, *as* Baſilius *ſeems to indicate, you can effect nothing; becauſe it hath already loſt its moſt ſubtle Sulphur in the firſt Diſtillation) grind it to ſo ſubtle a Powder, as it may paſs through a Tiffany Seive : put it into a* Cucurbit, *and pour upon it* Vinegar, *which according to Art is diſtilled from its proper* Minera. *Set it in Digeſtion for forty Days, and (if you have exactly obſerved all things,which are hereunto required)your Vinegar will be tinged with a Colour red as Blood. This red Tincture poured off by Inclination, put into a Retort, and gently abſtract the Vinegar. The Powder remaining extract with ſpirit of Wine, that it alſo may contract a blood-like Colour. Put this Extraction into a Circulatory Veſſel, like to this, the Figure of which I here expoſe ;*

Here place the Figure in the 96 Page.

becauſe I never found any more apt to render the Spirits volatile : Then place

The

this double Veſſel in B. M. *to be digeſted ſo long, as until you ſee the Tincturā raiſe it ſelf upwards and paß over volatile by Alembeck; ſeeing this, cool your Veſſel, and put all the Matter into a* Cucurbit, *and diſtil the Spirit according to Art, which will paß over the Helm as red as Blood. Then again abſtract the Spirit, and you will have a moſt ponderous thick Oyl.*

How this Oyl ſhould after this be joyned with its own Salt, and united, we elſewhere ſpeak; the uſe of which in amending Metals is very great. Here we have deſcribed it, and brought it ſo far, as It becomes a moſt excellent Medicine in grievous Diſeaſes, which are in all places accounted uncurable.. It performs its whole Operation by Sweats. And ſince there is no Diſeaſe, which it helps not; what need is there to name any? It is better to be altogether Silent, then to detract from its praiſes, by reciting a few. There is no man who hath made any Progreß in Chymiſtry, that knows not what the Quinteſſence *of* Antimony *is.*

The *Phyſician* before all Things, ſhould diligently contemplate its uſe, according to his own Experience and Knowledge; but eſpecially compleating its Preparation in a due manner, without being weary of his labour, or forgetting any of thoſe Things which are preſcribed to be performed.

Again, another Extraction of *Antimony*, is thus inſtituted. Take, in the Name of the Lord, of *Antimony* and crude *Tartar*, of each equal parts; put theſe well mixed together in Powders, into a ſtrong Crucible, which will not ſuffer the Spirits to penetrate it, and burn this Matter in the Fire, until the *Tartar* be wholy combuſt : this work muſt be done in a Wind-Fornace. Grind this burnt Matter to a ſubtle Powder, and pour on that Common Water firſt made hot, and ſo edulcorate the Matter by Lixiviating. And ſo it becomes a *Liver*[*], ſo called by many of our Anceſtors, who lived long before us.

---

[*] *The* Liver *is a Cauſe of much Diſcourſe in Banquets, and the* Liver *of Antimony will be to us no ſmall Occaſion of the like in Chymical Operations. But in the firſt place conſider, than inſtead of Crude Tartar, it is better to take Salt of Tartar, not only for accelerating the Operation (for otherwiſe it muſt be*

melted ſo long, as until the Tartar be changed into Salt) but chiefly, that you may have Glaſs of a far better Colour. Alſo Baſilius *forgot, or for ſome Reaſons did omit, to appoint the Glaſs firſt to be poured into a Platter made hot, and then beaten to powder in an hot Mortar: otherwiſe the Glaſs, by reaſon of the Salt of Tartar, as ſoon as it takes the cold Air is changed into a certain Pulſe or Pap. Beſides, he omitted to determine the Quantity of Water, in which this Powder ſhould be diſſolved, that we may have a more fair and deep Colour; in which Exaltation of Colour very much is ſited. Alſo the Precipitatton of the* Liver *from the water, which muſt be made with Vinegar, he involved in Silence; although this, and the above mentioned, are neceſſary in this Operation.*

Here I am unwilling to forbear to admoniſh, that not only in this, but in every Melting of Antimony, the Artiſt ought to obſerve the Face of Heaven, and begin his Work when the ſame is clear and ſerene. If you do otherwiſe, you will in vain deplore the Obſcurity of the Colour in your Liver of *Antimony. For if you laugh at me, attributing much Virtue to the Influences of the Stars, I ſhall deride you, deploring the unluckie Succeſs of many Proceſſes. But I would not digreſs ſo far, as to take on me to prove the Virtues of Celeſtial Influences, againſt men, either knowing ſo little, as they cannot underſtand, or having experienced ſomewhat do not diſcern; but in the mean while are ſo obſtinate, as they will not believe thoſe things which they ſee, have tried, and in very deed found to be ſo. I would no more urge Reaſons againſt theſe men, then againſt theſe, who deny even the Mutation of Metals by the* Stone of Philoſophers. *We judge ſuch men more worthy of Contempt than Refutation, who ſay that is not poſſible, which they have beheld with their Eyes, and done with their hands; for it is very rude to ſay,* I deny, I deny, *who proves? Theſe perverſe men by their thus acting, do ſometimes provoke the patience of good ingenious Artiſts, judging that they, with a certain Zeal of confirming what they aſſert, will proceed ſo far, as to diſcover to them their Experiment of ſo excellent an Art. But I do not think that any of them, who have obtained the Myſtery will be ſo imprudent, as unadviſedly to caſt Pearls before Swine, and to diſcover to th Unworthy, what* GOD *hath revealed to him; or give them of the Bread h Eats, which is not to be caſt to Dogs.*

Therefore, returning to the Matter from whence I digreſſed, I affirm, that ther are ſometimes of the year, in which if Liver of *Antimony be made, and pre cipitated with a due* Menſtruum, *it will be imbibed with altogether anothe Colour, and be endued with other Virtues than that, which is made at anothe time; and that, both for Metals, and for healing the Infirmities of men, as I m ſelf have experienced in many grievous Diſeaſes, and Symptoms of Diſeaſes. will alſo add this: from the* Liver of Antimony *may be extracted a Redne with Spirit of Wine, which Redneſs is made volatile, and paſſeth over th Helm, which alſo may be exhibited to all without danger. Nor is there a great need of that Caution of* Baſilius *(even before the Redneſs is volatilized that it muſt be given in a ſmall Quantity. For being given from thirty forty, or fifty Drops, it ſweats very moderately, and doth not Purge or Vomit*

Ɩ

but it effects wonders in purging the Blood, extirpating the Roots of a Disease, and rendring the Patient vigorous, by insensible Expiration, and its occult Virtues. This Vendible Wine needs not the Bush of Eloquence to commend it to the Sick; who once having experienced its Virtues, know what it can do, and that it as much answers their Desires, as they esteem their Money.

Put this Liver dried into a *Cucurbit*, pour thereon most pure Spirit of Wine; abstract the Spirit by distilling in *B. M.* so that a third part only may remain. But before Distillation, the Spirit of Wine together with the Extraction must be filtred through Paper. This Extraction may indeed be profitably used; but in a small Dose, and with great Caution. What happens in this Operation is very admirable. For the Spirit of Wine abstracted, can no more be united with the red Extraction, whence it was distilled; but one floats above the other, as Water and Oyl, which cannot be mixed. But if the abstracted Spirit of Wine be poured upon other Liver of *Antimony*, it again attracts the Colour to it self; yet this, although poured upon the former Extraction, cannot be mixed therewith. Which is a Thing so strange, as it may be numbred among Wonders. But who can declare all the Wonders of *G O D ?* or who will worthily esteem the Gifts of the Creator, which he hath implanted in his Creatures? by us scarcely perscrutable with deep Meditation.

I before made mention of the Extraction of *Antimony*, from its Glass * by Vinegar, and also by Spirit of Wine: but now I say, when such an Extraction is made by Vinegar, and the Vinegar is again abstracted by *B. M.* and the Powder which remains is resolved in a moist place, into Oyl or Liquor of a Yellow Colour; it effects such Wonders in Wounds, new and old, as I neither can, nor dare to commit them all to writing.

** Here our Author acts as a Teacher careful, and full of Affection, who not
fatisfied once to mention, doth often inculcate the principal Precepts of his Doctrine.
But, what it is, that Specially moves him to repeat the Virtues of the Sulphur of
Antimony, I fee not : he faith, he repeats nothing in vain; therefore do thou,
Reader, if thou judgeft it of Concern, more attently confider, whether you may
not here find fomewhat that is not mentioned, or the Reafon why it is again
Spoken of. I, who profefs my felf to write to the Intelligent, reiterate nothing
here. He that comprehends, let him comprehend ; he that hath not there under-
ftood, I fear will not here underftand.*

For it reprefleth all Symptoms of what kind fo
ever, fuffereth none to take Root, and admits no
Putrefaction in frefh Wounds. Alfo the Extraction of this Powder, before Solution is made by Spirit of Wine, effects the fame, and yields not us inferiour to other Medicaments, which are admini-
ftred againft internal Affects.

I have often made mention of this Preparation
in other of my Writings, alfo in this Treatife of
Antimony, very largely ; becaufe I know how great
Benefits and how great Secrets are latent in it.
Therefore I hope, no Difciple will be affected with
tedioufnefs, by Reafon of Repetitions in my Writings, which I faithfully open and bring to Light.
For whatfoever I write is not without Reafon ;
and my words are Short, but require much Confi-
deration, although often repeated. To the Ignorant my Difcourfes contribute little underftanding,
to Children and the unexperienced little Profit ;
but to my Difciples and Apoftles, much health and
profperity.

There remains another Extraction by a Cauftick
Water, which Experience hath taught me in this
manner.

Take of Vitriol and Common Salt, equal parts ;
from thefe by Retort diftil a Water ***, which being forced out by vehement fire, comes forth a
matter

matter like thin Butter, or the Sediment of Oyl
Olive; which keep apart for use.

** Here I will teach you the Manual Operation, O Lover of Chymistry, which
undoubtedly you will greatly esteem of, when you shall find the great commo-
dity thereof in operating. Lest, as it often happens, when you distil the Spirits of Metals, your Vessels should be broken.*

Here place the Figure in the 101 Page.

*Of your Earthen Retort A. open the upper hole B. into which put your Matter
by Parts, lest all together senting the heat, should act too forcibly; and presently close the Hole with its proper Cover. To the Spirits received in the Vessel
C. exit is given by the hole D. into the other opposit Receiver E. to which again
is applied the other Receiver F. So, the more subtle Spirits ascending through
the Hole D, settle in the Recipient F. But the more gross remain in the bottom G.
of the Receiver C. This Instrument will be most apt for your use here; not
only, as I said, lest a most strong Spirit passing out break the Glasses, but also
for other works, as by an easie speculation you will hence gather.*

Subtly grind the *Caput-mortuum*, and in a Cellar
permit it to resolve into Water, this Water keep
and filter it through Paper. Afterward take *Hungarian Antimony*, grind it to a fine Powder, and
having put it in a *Cucurbit* with a flat bottom,
pour this Water thereon, and set the Vessel in
Heat. When it hath stood there for a due time,
the Matter will be like an *Amethyst*, with a blackish
Violet-Colour. Then augment the Fire much,
and you will have a transparent Colour, like unto
a blew *Saphyr*. From this Colour precipitate a white
Powder, by pouring on Common Water. This
Powder taken, hath the same Operation, as the
Red Extraction of Glass of *Antimony*, by Seidge,
and it also excites Vomiting. In that Solution
made from the *Caput-mortuum*, and kept in a Cellar,
if thin Plates of Iron be digested, *Mars* will be
truly transmuted into *Venus*, as Experience will
teach.

Now further consider. Take that distilled Oyl

H 3   or

or Water, as is fpoken of above in this procefs,
and pour it upon *Crocus Martis*, with *Sulphur* re-
verberated to a Rednefs; fet the Mixture in Heat,
and you will have an extracted Tincture of *Mars*,
red as blood.   Take of this Extraction one part;
of the Red Extraction of *Antimony*, which is prepared with fixed Salt Nitre and Spirit of Wine,
three Parts; of the Water of *Mercury* * leifurely
injected through a long Pipe, one Part;

* Chymifts, *that they may whet the Ingenuities of their Readers ; and
more, left any but the true Students of Art fhould penetrate into their Secrets,
deliver not all Things in one place, but fcatter their Documents, that by the Diligent Collection of them, they may judge of their Aptnefs, as the Eagle proves
her Young, expofing them to the Solar Rays : fo you fee* Bafilius *here propofeth
the ufe of the Water of* Mercury, *which he taught to be made in his Treatife,
which is Call'd a Supplement, or rather gave a rude Draught of that Procefs.
For neither there, nor here doth he make mention of an hole, that muft be open,
in the fuperior part of the Retort, and thereinto a long Pipe fitted , through
which the* Mercury *may be put in, in very fmall Parcels.   For if you include
a very fmall part of* Mercury *in a Retort, firft made very hot with a vehement Fire, as this muft be, if you would extract the Spirit, that* Mercury,
*with its own vehement and untamable violence, would not only burft the Retort,
but overthrow the Fornace alfo ; unlefs you give it a larger Space, and greater
liberty of Flying ; fo that, after it hath rifted many Retorts, it may reft, and
being as it were tired, fettle.   But fince it is well known to all true* Chymifts,
of how great Virtue this Mercury *is, in the Refolution of Metals, I will here
make no farther mention thereof.*

and of the Calx of Gold diffolved in this Cauftick
Water, half a part.   Mix all thefe together , and
after they are canted off clear, diftil the Mixture
with a Moderate Fire in Sand.   All will not pafs
over by Diftillation, but a fair clear Solution remains fixed * in the Bottom; which we may ufe in
old open Wounds, wherein it laies a Foundation
for Healing to Amazement.

* *This Solution is not yet fixed, but if you be not already wearied with
labour , by a farther Operation you may fix it. The principal ufe of this is,*

The

in the Emendation of Metals, which Basilius *doth doth not so much as mention. Now the* Genius *of all* Chymists *will understand me, here candidly discovering this* Secret *to all.* Do thou, Lover *of* Chimistry, *in mind and thought swiftly follow me expounding the Oracle; but the Operation cannot be so swiftly performed.*

This Powder must first be Extracted *n i b strong Vinegar, which afterward abstract, and what remains in the bottom edulcorate with distilled water: again* Extract *it with* Spirit *of Wine, and abstract the* Spirit, *and in the bottom will remain a Red Powder.* Joyn *this with the fixed Salt, which is made of the* Feces, *which remained after the* Vinegar *was used for* Extraction. *And deliver it to* Vulcan *for three Months space, that it may no more flie from the Fire, but most pleasingly sport with and in the same. If you perform this, you have* Two *conjoyned in an inseparable* Matrimony: *and you have separated the pure from the impure, have rendred the* Volatile *fixed, and fixed the* Volatile, *and are not far from that* Felicity, *which will answer all your Desires.*

The *Caput mortuum* which is left, being resolved in an Humid place, yields a Liquor so sharp, as no *Aqua fortis* may be compared with it in Sharpnes. But of these enough at this time. For I must now speak of a White Powder, which may also be prepared of *Antimony* in this manner.

Take pure *Antimony*, which is brought from *Hungaria*, or found in like Mountainous Places; grind it to a subtle Powder: take also the same measure of pure Salnitre, which hath been the third time diligently cleansed. This Composition burn in a new glazed Pot (which was never infected with any Fatness) in a Circulatory Fire; not all together, but by parts, and at divers times. This way of Operating, Ancient *Spagyrists* called *Detonation*, a Term of Art to be learned by the Disciple of Art, as being not Common to every Rustick, in his Artifice and Experience.

This Operation being performed, grind the hard Matter, which remained in the Pot, to a fine Powder, and upon it in another Glazed Pot pour common Water warm; which when the Matter is setled again repeat the pouring on of Water several times, until all the Salnitre be extracted:

Lastly,

Lastly, dry the remaining Matter, and with fresh Salnitre * as much as its own weight is, burn it again, and repeat the same Operation 'the third time.

* Basilius doth not misguide or delude you, O Lover of Chymistry, whilst he so candidly discovers most Secret Mysteries, and so sincerely and faithfully presents their wonderful Effects. As by this very Operation you have an Example: For after the first Detonation with Nitre, and so soon as you shall have separated the Salnitre from the Powder with pure Water, you have the Powder of Ruland, with which that man effected so many Medicinal Wonders, whereby he got to himself so great a Name, and so much Wealth. Which, if you prepare under a certain Constitution of Heaven (as I advised, in preparing the Liver of Antimony) you will have so much the better, by how much the more Red: for the Colour is the Soul thereof, the Effect of which in Medicine, Ruland proved and commended; but he, neither exhausted its prayses, nor did he perswade the unexperienced, that so great Virtues were latent in this Medicament. This Crocus of Metals (for so it is called) is not that, which is publickly sold in Shops, upon eight Grains of which they pour ℥ij. of Wine, and although the Sick only drink that wine, without any other Powder, it oftentimes works so forcibly, upwards and downwards, as either way, sometimes both wayes, the life it self issues out. But the use of this is thus. Take eight, nine, ten, or eleven Granes of this our Author's preparing the first Time, according to the strength of the Sick, and all other Things co-indicating; pour on them three or four ounces of Wine; for it matters not much, whether you take more or less of the Wine. Set the Mixture in B. M. for the space of four or five hours, and so extract a most Red Tincture from this Crocus of Metals (which in an Infusion of the Crocus of the Shops cannot be extracted) this Wine, now impregnated with the Sulphur of the Crocus, together with the more subtle part of the Powder, which in casting off comes out, I give to the Sick, and it purgeth kindly upwards and downwards without molestation. Nor doth this Medicament only expel Humours, but (as is proper to Antimonials rightly prepared) it strikes at the very Root of the Disease, and whatsoever in the Body is corrupted and declined from its due state, that it amends and restores. What wonderful Effects, this only Tincture hath discovered to me, I forbear to mention, lest I should be compelled to bring their Credit in Question, who have experienced them. In this only believe me, whosoever thou art, that wouldest use Chymical Medicaments, alwayes be sure to take the true Tinctures of Things, in which their volatile Sulphur is absconded; if you neglect this, you neglect your own Fame and Gain, and the Health of the Sick.

What remains after this third Operation grind to a subtle Powder, and on that pour the best Spirit

rit of Wine; circulate the Mixture for one Month, in a Cucurbit or Circulatory diligently nine or ten times, so often pouring on fresh Spirit. This being done, dry the Powder with gentle heat, and for one whole Day keep it red-hot in a Crucible, such as Goldsmiths use to melt their Metals in. Afterward resolve this Powder (in a moyst Place, upon a Stone or Glafs Table, or in Eggs boyled to an hardnefs) into a Liquor, which set in heat, again dry, and reduce to Powder. This Powder effects many egregious and wonderful Things, which cannot easily be believed by Those, who have not proved the same. *

If you have believed, or experienced the Virtues of this Powder once detonated, you will not be a Thomas *in this third Detonation. Set to your hand, touch and use this, and it will perform the same, which true* Diaphoretick Antimony *can, but with greater Security and Efficacy.*

But it operates not suddenly, it must have time to exercise its Powers, and shew its own Vertue, by the Testimony of Experience, very admirable.

Whosoever labours with internal Imposthumes, let him take of this white fixed Powder of *Antimony* in the Spirit of Wine, or any other rich Wine, the fourth part of a Dram, five or six times a Day, and he will find his internal Imposthume opened, and all the Coagulated Blood to be expelled by degrees, without any peril of Life or Health. He, who is afflicted in his Body with the New Disease of Souldiers, if he use this Powder in the aforesaid manner, will also find this Evil consumed throughout the whole Body, and by the same expelled. Moreover, it produceth new Hairs, and renovates a man to the admiration of all men; it gives new, sound, and pure Blood, and is the Effecter of so much Good, as even the least part of it (although

Equity

Equity feems to require this) cannot by me be defcribed or declared. It is not fit I fhould here manifeft all things clearly, and in fuch manner, as any
man, without Labour and Toyl, by reading my
Writings, may become a perfect *Doctor*; no more
than it is fit, that a *Young Country Man* * fhould be
fed with the whiteft and beft baked Bread, which
he hath not prepared with his own Labour, or the
Corn of which himfelf thrafhed not out.

* *Valentine hath fo clearly detected all Things, as no man, either before or
after him, hath done it more clearly. All that came after him feem to have con-
fpired, and agreed together to fpread Clouds over that Light, which he brought
into the World. Hence it is, that they do not Publickly extol his Prayfes, according to the high Efteem every man Privately hath of him ; nor have they
tranflated his Books into other Tongues, although He?, of all Authors, is the moft
worthy, who fpeaks in the Languages of all Nations, that he may be a comfort
to the Lovers of Chymiftry, erring in the Labyrinths of others, and always
produce a new Off-fpring of Philofophers. But no man fhould think, that he
could fo clearly fpeak, as every man, handling Chymiftry (according to the
Saying) with unwafhed Hands, might prefently underftand him ; that is, as
himfelf faith, not poffible to be done, nor is it expedient that the Son of a vile
Clown fhould eat of the fineft Flower, in preparing which he took no Pains ;
yet (as below he confeffeth) our Author hath ufed plain, fimple and clear
words.*

But I make too large a Progrefs in this open
Field of Doctrine, in which the Ancient Hunters
take their Larks, and the Young Ones prefently
follow them with their Nets. For my Style(as all my
Writings witnefs) hath a certain fingular purpofed Method, like that of all Philofopers before me.
If any one think it ftrange, that I here propofe
certain fingular Proceffes, in which my Philofophy
differs from other, let him be anfwered with this,
that Philofophick Speech much differs from the
Method of other mens Difcourfes, who nakedly
and fincerely declare fome Procefs, without any
Ambiguities or Cloudings of *Ænigma's*. Therefore, confider the difference, and accufe not me,

as if I had deviated from Order, in my Style of Philofophy , and of Preparations and Procefles. For in a Philofophick Difcourfe, it is behooful to learn and judge of what appertains to the Theory, but the Practice teacheth you the Inftruction of Procefles; therefore in them, true, fimple, clear and well grounded Words are to be ufed.

Alfo , of *Antimony* is made a *Balfom*, againft grievous Difeafes very profitable ; yet not of Crude *Antimony* , but of the *Regulus* thereof, whence may be made living *Mercury* , in the following manner.

Take of the beft *Hungarian Antimony*, and crude * Tartar equal parts, and of Salnitre half a part ; grind them well together, and afterward flux them in a Wind-Furnace ; pour out the flowing Matter into a Cone , and there let it cool ; then you will find the *Regulus*, which thrice or oftner purge by Fire, with Tartar and Nitre, and it will be bright and white, fhining like Cupellate Silver, which hath fulminated and overcome all its Lead.

---

* *What I advifed to in the Preparation of* Liver *of* Antimony *is here to be repeated ; inftead of Crude Tartar take Salt of Tartar, by which the Operation will fooner and better proceed. Salnitre here is unprofitable. Therefore, take of* Antimony *and Salt of Tartar, of each equal parts, melt them and make a Regulus, according to the Rule here given by* Bafilius. *If you caft away the Glafs (as all men for the moft part do) you will do ill. For I, of that prepare a very profitable Medicament in this manner. I grind this Glafs in an hot Mortar, taking heed it contract no Humidity from the Air, which may eafily be prevented , and having put it in a Phial , pour Alcohol of Wine thereon, and thence extract a moft beautiful Tincture, in Colour red like Blood. This Tincture is a moft excellent Cordial, if thirty, forty or fifty Drops of it be taken in convenient Liquor, and that, if you will, twice or thrice a day ; for it is taken with fafety, and recreates the whole Man.*

Grind this *Regulus* to a fubtle Powder, and having put it into a Glafs, pour it on Oyl of Juniper, or Spirit of Turpentine, which comes forth in the

fir ft

firſt Diſtillation, and is pure as Fountain Water;
keep the Veſſel well cloſed, in a ſubtle heat of *B.
M.* and the Oyl of Juniper, or Spirit of Turpentine, will become red as Blood, which pour off,
and rectifie with Spirit of Wine. This is endued with the ſame Virtues, as Balſom of Sulphur, as
I ſhall then ſhew, when I write of Sulphur, becauſe
they require one and the ſame Preparation.

Of this Balſom only three or four Drops, taken
thrice in a Week with hot Wine, heal the Diſeaſes
of the Lungs, cure the frequent Cough, and *Aſth-
ma,* alſo they are conducent in the *Vertigo,* prickings of the Sides and in diuturnal Coughs.

Alſo many Oyls may be prepared of *Antimony,*
ſome *per ſe* and without Addition, and many others
by Addition. Yet they are not endued with the
ſame Virtues, but each enjoys its own, according
to the Diverſity of its Preparation. Of which I
now give you this Similitude. There are many
kinds of Animals, which live only in the Earth, as
are many Creeping Things, Worms and Serpents;
alſo others, ſome of which are new kinds, which
before were not, and theſe alſo proceed from Putrefaction of the Earth. Some inhabit the Waters, as all kinds of Fiſhes; others flie through
the Air, as every kind of Flying Things, and Birds;
ſome alſo are nouriſhed in the Fire, as the Salamander. And beſides theſe, in the more hot Re-
gions and Iſlands, are found many other Animals,
which to theſe Nations are unknown, which prolong their Life by the Solar Heat, and which die
ſo ſoon as brought into another Air. So *Antimony,* when prepared by the Addition of Water,
aſſumes another Nature and Complexion for operating, then when prepared by Fire only. And
although every Preparation of it ought to be
made by Fire, without which the Virtue of it cannot

not be manifefted : yet confider, that the Addition of Earth gives it wholly another Nature, than
the Addition of Water. So alfo when *Antimony*
is fublimed in Fire through the Air , and further
prepared, another Virtue, other Powers, and another Operation follow , than in the Preparations
already defcribed. Therefore the Oyl of *Antimony*, *per fe*, without addition , and the true Sulphur thereof are prepared after this Method.

Take crude *Hungarian Antimony*, put that ground
to a fubtle Powder, into a Glafs *Cucurbit* with a
flat bottom: and pour thereon the true Vinegar
of Philofophers rendred more acid with its own
Salt. Then fet the *Cucurbit* firmly clofed in Horfe-
dung, or *B. M.* to putrefie the matter for forty
Days, in which time the Body refolves it felf, and
the Vinegar contracts a Colour red as Blood.
Pour off the Vinegar , and pour on frefh, and do
this fo often, as until the Vinegar can no more be
tinged. This being done, filtre all the Vinegar
through Paper, and again fet it, put into a clean
Glafs firmly clofed again in Horfe-dung, or *B. M.*
as before, that it may putrefie for forty Days; in
which time the Body again refolves it felf, and the
Matter in the Glafs becomes as black as *Calcan-
thum* , or Shoomakers Ink. When you have this
Sign, then true Solution is made, by which the further Separation of Elements is procured. Put
this black matter into another Cucurbit, to which
apply an Alembick, and diftil off the Vinegar with
moderate Fire ; then the Vinegar paffeth out
clear, and in the bottom a fordid matter remains ;
grind that to a fubtle Powder , and edulcorate it
with diftilled Rain Water, then dry it with gentle
heat, and put it a Circulatory with a long Neck
(the Circulatory muft have three Cavities or Bel-
lics, as if three Globes were fet one above another,

: yet

yet diftinct or apart each from other, as Sublima-
tories, with their Aludel [or Head] are wont to
be made, and it muft have a long Neck like a Phial,
(or Bolthead and pour on it Spirit of Wine highly rectified, till it rifeth three Fingers above the
Matter, and having well clofed the Veffel , fet it
in a moderate heat for two Months.   Then follows another new Extraction , and the Spirit of
Wine becomes tranfparently red as a Ruby, or as
was the firft Extraction of the Vinegar , yea more
fair.   Pour off the Spirit of Wine thus tinged,
filtre it through Paper, and put it into a Cucurbit
(the black Matter which remains fet afide, and feparate from this Work; for it is not profitable
therein) to which apply an Head and Receiver,
and having firmly clofed all Junctures, begin to
diftil in Afhes with moderate Fire : then the Spirit
of wine carries over the Tincture of *Antimony* with
it felf, the Elements feparate themfelves each from
other , and the Alembeck and Recipient feem to
refemble the form of pure Gold tranfparent in
Afpect.   In the end fome few Feces remain, and the
Golden Colour in the Glafs altogether fayls.   The
red Matter, which in diftilling paffed over into the
Receiver, put into a Circulatory for ten Days,
and as many Nights.   By that Circulation Separation is made ; for the Oyl thereby acquires Gra-
vity, and feparates it felf to the bottom from the
Spirit of Wine; and the Spirit of Wine is again
Clear, as it was at firft, and fwims upon the Oyl.
Which admirable Separation is like a Miracle in
Nature : Separate this Oyl * from the Spirit of
Wine by a Separatory.

---

* *Here you have not only whatfoever can be made of* Antimony *, but alfo
almoft all that can be promifed by a* Chymift. *This is that with which all the*

This

Books of all Chymists are filled, which is involved in so many Fables, compli-
cated in so many Riddles, and explicated with so many obscure Commentaries,
that is, which in all the World is desired by Fools, sought by the Sons of Art, and
found by the Wise. This Basilius reveals, this he repeats, this he inculcates;
this is his Triumphant Chariot, which he as it were carries about, and often
shews in the various Parts of his Writings. Before in this Treatise, he presents
it under the Name of an Extraction of Crude Antimony, here it is Oyl of Antimony, soon after it is converted into a Stone, which is called the Stone of Fire.
Thus this Proteus often offers it self, always various, yet always the same in
Substance. Compare all these Processes, which are so often diversly propounded,
with these my Commentaries made upon the Extraction of Crude Antimony,
and you will have the Work compleat in all its Numbers; you will have a Trea-
sure, in which, if you know not what you have, I remit you to Æsop's Dunghil-
Cock, who found a Gem in the Dunghil, but knew not wha' he had. Consider
diligently, O Lover of Chymistry, and you will find that no man hath dealt
more clearly and sincerly with Thee, than Basilius, and me after him, who shew
thee where the Hare !lies, which so many Others have hunted in vain. If now
you be not here wise, you will not be healed with three Anticyra's. Therefore I
will add nothing, lest I make Fools mad, who now indeed are wise.

This Oyl is of a singular and incredible Sweet-
nefs, with which no other thing may be compared,
it is grateful in the Ufe, and all Corrofivenefs is feparated from it. No man can by Cogitation
judge, by Underftanding comprehend, what incredible Effects, potent Powers, and profitable Virtues are in this Royal Oyl. Therefore, to this
Sulphur of *Antimony*, I have given no other Name,
than my Balfom of Life; becaufe it effects very
much, by the Grace of *G O D*, in thofe, in whom
was no help to be hoped for, but by the Mercy of
G O D, and nothing remained but a moft certain
expectation of changing Life with Death; as my
Brethren can witnefs hath been often done. It
refrefheth a man fo, as if he were new born; it
purifies the Blood; mixt and exhibited with the
Tincture of Corals, it cleanfeth the Leprofie, and
expels every Scab, which through impurity of
the Blood takes Root in man. It drives away
Melancholy and fadnefs of Heart, it confirms the
Junctures,

Junctures, and above all ftrengthens the Heart, when given with the Magiftery of Pearls. Alfo it helps the Memory, and in Swouning a more noble Medicine is not found, if fix drops of it mixt with equal parts of Oyl of Cinnamon be put upon the Tongue, and the Noftrils and Arteries be anointed with a little of the Effence of Saffron.

Ah Good *G O D*, what moves me to fpeak, write, and invent many Things! For I fuppofe I fhall find few among the *Doctors*, who will give abfolute Credit to thefe my Writings, which I have declared faithfully, inftead of a Teftament, to my Difciples, Apoftles, and Followers; but Others, who before knew thefe wonderful Effects, and have often in Truth experienced thefe Virtues, will more accurately attend, and more eafily believe, and for this bounty of mine *(viz.* becaufe I have opened, by the permiffion of *G O D*, the Powers and Virtues which are infufed in the Creatures, and have as it were freed them from Prifon, brought them to Light, and unto free Operation) give me thanks, and fpeak honourably of me, after I am reduced to Duft in the Grave.

Another way to drive *Antimony*, without Addition, over by Alembeck is this.

Make a *Regulus* of *Antimony*, by *Tartar* and *Salnitre*, as I above taught, grind this fubtily, put it in a great round Glafs, and place it in a moderate heat of Sand. This way the *Antimony* will be fublimed: whatfoever fhall be fublimed, that dayly put down with a Feather, that at length it may remain in the Bottom, and there perfift until nothing more of it can be fublimed, but the whole remains fixed in the Bottom. Then is your *Regulus* fixed and precipitated *per fe.* But confider, here is required a fufficient time, and repetition of the Labour often, before you can obtain that. This Red Precipitate

cipitate take out, grind it to a fubtle Powder,
which fpred upon a flat and clean Stone, fet in a
cold moift Place and there let it remain for fix
Months; at length the Precipitate begins to refolve it felf into a red and pure Liquor, and the
Feces or Earth is feparated from it. The Salt of
Antimony, I fay, only refolves it felf into Liquor,
which filter, and put into a Cucurbit, that it may
be condenfed by extraction of the phlegm; and
again fet it in a moyft place, then will it yield you
fair Cryftals. Separate thefe from their phlegm,
and they will be pellucid, mixt wiith a red Colour;
but when again purified become white. Then is
made the true Salt * of *Antimony*, as I have often
prepared it.

* Ἴσ῀ ἴσ῀. or like with like, *is a Proverb among the Greeks, and is
here manifeft in our Chymical Work. For this Salt acuates all* Menftruum's;
for their more eafie extraction of Metals; but thofe Extractions moft, which
are made of Antimony, *as of a Mineral to it of affinity and like.*

This Salt dry, and mix with it *Venenian* Earth
(which is called *Tripel*) three Parts, and in ftrong
Fire diftil it. Firft a white Spirit comes off, afterward a red Spirit, which alfo refolves it felf into
white. Rectifie this Spirit gently and fubtily in
a dry or moyft *Balneo*, and fo you will have another white Oyl diftilled from the Salt of *Antimony*.
This Oyl, but why do I call it Oyl? this Spirit, I
fhould rather fay, fince the Salt is diftilled in a
Spiritual manner, in Quartans and other Feavers
often manifefts its Virtues, and is very conducent
in breaking the Stone of the Bladder; it provokes
Urine, and is profitable in the Gout. Outwardly
applied to old corrofive Wounds, which have their
Operation from *Mars*, it purifies them. Alfo,
this Spirit of the Salt of *Antimony* purifies the
whole Blood, as the Salt of Gold doth. And al-

though.

though , in healing very many other Difeafes it
may be profitably applied, yet it is not fo perfect,
as the above defcribed red Oyl of *Antimony*, in
which its Sulphur is deduced to the higheft, purified and feparated, as I faid ; therefore I forbear
to fpeak more of this.

Now , fince I have treated of the Sulphur and
Salt of *Antimony*, and fhewed how they may be reduced into Oyl and Spirit, to be fubfervient to
Medicine ; I here treating further , purpofe to
fpeak of its *Mercury* alfo, and to manifeft what
Medicine lies abfconded , and as it were buried
in it.

Take the *Regulus* of *Antimony*, made in fuch
manner, as I above taught, eight Parts.   Salt of
Humane Urine clarified and fublimed , one Part.
Sal-Armoniack one Part : and one Part of Salt of
Tartar.   Mix all the Salts together in a Glafs, and
having poured on ftrong Wine-Vinegar , lute it
with the Luting of Sapience, and digeft the Salts
with the Vinegar for an intire Moneth in convenient Heat ; afterward put all into a Cucurbit, and
in Afhes diftil off the Vinegar, that the Salts may
remain dry.   Thefe dry Salts mix with three Parts
of *Venetian* Earth, and by Retort diftil the Mixture with ftrong Fire, and you will have a wonderful Spirit.   This Spirit pour upon the aforefaid
Regulus of *Antimony* reduced to Powder , and fet
the whole in putrefaction for two Moneths.   Then
gently diftil the Vinegar from it, and with what
remains mix a fourfold weight of the filings of
Steel, and with violent Fire diftil by Retort : then,
the Spirit of Salt, which paffeth out, carries over
with it felf the *Mercury* of *Antimony* in the Species of Fume.   Wherefore in this Operation you
muft apply a great Recipient with a large quantity
of Water in it, fo doing, the Spirit of Salt will be
mixed

mixed with the Water, but the *Mercury* collected in the Bottom of the Glass into true Living *Mercury.* *

* *what were* Arcanum's *in the times of* Basilius, *are now in our times but vulgar Chymical Works. How often shall we find any One, who numbers him-self among true* Chymists, *that is ignorant of the Way of making* Mercury *of* Antimony? *either in this manner, as* Basilius *teacheth, or in another. For various Artificers have now invented various Methods, and every One useth that, he best approves of.*

Behold, O Lover of Art, I have shewed you, how of *Antimony* may be made Running *Mercury*, which very many have so long, and in so many Parts of the World sought; and how we may use this *Mercury* with prayse in Medicine, I will here discover and set down in Writing:

Take in the Name of the Lord, of this *Mercury* one Part, expreſs it through a Skin, and pour on it of red Oyl of Vitriol highly rectified, four Parts. Extract the Oyl, and the Spirits of the Oyl will remain with the *Mercury:* Force it with vehement Fire, and somewhat will be sublimed. This Sublimate again put down upon the Earth in the Bottom. Then pour on other Oyl, of the same weight as before, and repeat this labour a third time. The fourth time, put the Sublimate which ascends with the Earth, and grind both together, and the whole will be clear and pure, like a *Speculum* or Cryſtal. Put this into a Circulatory, and pour on it a like weight of Oyl of Vitriol, and thrice so much Spirit of Wine. Circulate until Separation be made, and at length the *Mercury* resolve it self into Oyl, and float about like Oyl Olive. When you see this, separate this Oyl from the other Liquor, and put it into a Circulatory, and there pour on ſtrong diſtilled Vinegar, and permit it so to reſt for about twenty Days. Then this Oyl again acquires its own Gravity, and settles to the

Bottom; and whatfoever Venenofity was in it, remains in the Vinegar, which will be tenebrous and altogether confufed. *

There is no need of Torches at Noon Day, nor of Commentaries in so perspicuous a Description, by which Basilius teacheth to make the Mercury of Antimony. Begin leifurely, give heed to all particulars, and your Work shall never deceive you. Left I should darken the Author, I defift from Commenting; but add, that I doubt not, but that this Mercury will manifeft wonderful Effects in the Humane Body: Yet I have not experienced its Virtues for the health of Animals, therefore my Commentaries muft not exceed my Experience.

But in the Emendation of Metals, it shews it felf to be endued with fingular Virtues. For I fay, and clearly affirm, he that can bring this Oyl here defcribed by Basilius, *to the ftate of a fixed Stone, may glory that he hath a fixed Tincture, only inferior to the one only King of Kings, the Great ftone of Philofophers. When thou haft proceeded thus far, O Lover of Chymiftry, go not back, nor take off thy hand from the Plough: but go on chearfully, perhaps in fo great a Grave.*

The Golden Branch, with Leaves and Twigs of Gold
will shew it felf to Thee———

This is a great *Arcanum*, and feems repugnant to Nature, that this Oyl should firft fwim, and afterward being rendred more ponderous, fettle to the Bottom. But confider, the Oyl of Vitriol is alfo heavy, yet when the *Mercury* in its Separation is not altogether pure, it ftands above it; but when the impure Lightnefs is taken from it by Vinegar, becaufe the Vinegar affumes that, then the Oyl receives its juft weight, becomes compact, and fettles to the Bottom. This is the Oyl of the *Mercury* of *Antimony*, which is the fourth Column of Medicine.

Now come hither you Lepers! where be you? I will fupply you with Means for Health. This Oyl is profitable againft the Apoplexy, comforts the Brain, makes a man induftrious, and cherifheth the vital Spirits of the Head. If any one hath laboured long with grievous Difeafes, and will for
some

some time dayly ufe this Oyl, his Hairs and Nayls will fall off, and he will be renovated, as a man new-born. All the Blood in the Humane Body is by it fo purified, as every Evil is taken off from it, and expelled. This heals the *French Difeafe*, which we have lately inherited; for by this Medicine it is radically extirpated. And, to comprehend much in few words, the praife of this Oyl is greater in Medicine, than can be exprefled by Speech or Writing.

Why do we, miferable Mortals, taken from the Earth, and ready to return into Earth, ftick here? Why do we not haften to give Thanks to *G O D* our *Creator*, for this Medicine fo mercifully granted to Us? You *Doctors* (if it pleafe the Gods) of either Medicine, come to me a religious man and Servant of *G O D*, I will manifeft to you what your Eyes never faw, and will fhew you the way of Health and Sanity, which before you never knew. Yet if any one be found among you, who under-ftands my Procefles, and the way of Preparation, better than I; let him, I pray, not be filent, or fet a Seal to his Lips: for here I ftand ready to learn, nor am I afhamed further to inquire, and defire that Light, which before I knew not. For I have often faid, that this our Life is circumfcribed with more ftrait Limits, then that one man fhould be able to fearch out all Things, which Nature bears abfconded in her Bofom. But on the contrary, I being the Author, let them be filent, who have ex-perienced lefs than I, and if they have not attained to a folid Underftanding of my Writings, let them not attempt to amend them, or (like Braw-lers) with inconfiderate Words reprehend, what they never learned in the Schools, and the Procefles of which they never received from men skilled in the Law. For my Terms otherwife found, and

. fignifie

fignifie other than theirs, who oppofe themfelves
againft me, and who are afhamed of the Labour of
Planting Trees, and of Grafting fruitful Sprouts
thereon; therefore they always abide among dry
and withered Wild Trees, and can never attain to
any Branch of green, fappy, and well manured
Fruit Trees.

Haften not, I fay, O man experienced in our
Art, to pafs your Sentence of Judging, and be not
willing to condemn, what you have not yet your
felf acquired by Thoughts, or gained by Difci-
pline. Many imprudent men frequently fay, Fifhes
are frozen in Waters; but thefe difcover their
own imprudence and want of Knowledge. For
it will never be proved, that a Fifh, even in the
bittereft Winter will ever be frozen in Waters, as
long as the Ice of thofe Waters is dayly broken by
the diligence of Mortals. But the reafon why
Fifhes dye, is becaufe, when the Ice is not opened,
their refpiration is hindred, and they thence are
are fuffocated. For it may eafily be proved, that
no Animal can live, when to it the ufe of Air is
denied. Whence it may well be concluded, that
thofe Fifhes, which are found dead under the Water, in an extream Cold Seafon, die not of Cold (as
men of little underftanding think) but becaufe
they are deprived of Air. By like Reafon (that
we may apply this Example) I fay; fince *Antimony*,
is to produce fuch admirable Fruits, it is to be
taken out of the Mountains; but firft, by the Care
of the Miners fpiracles, or breathing places, are
to be made for it, and afterward it muft be prepared with Water, Air and Fire, as with auxiliary
Mediums, left its fruitfulnefs be fuffocated in the
Earth. But with many and laborious Preparations of Artifice, it muft be manifefted and brought
to Light, for the expected Sanation of Difeafes,

                                      by

by reason of which it hath been so long sought into.

Where now, O Wretch! who contemnest *Antimony*, and among all men accusest it as mere Venom, where is thy Rhetorick, or Dialect, wherewith to defend thy self? But since thou understandest neither White, nor Black, nor Green, nor Red, nor Yellow; nor knowest which way to go about to justifie *Antimony*, its Virtue, Power and Utility, being unknown to thee, thou doest well, if thou keepest Silence, and permittest this Reprehension of thy Ignorance, as a Wave driven with vehement wind to fly over thy Head; fearing, that if those Winds and Waves should be predominant, thy own weak and frail Bark would be sunk and submerged. To avoid this peril, seasonably call upon thy Sleeping Master, as the Disciples of our *Saviour Jesus Christ* did, when they feared they should perish. Yet this must not be done with a dissembled and feigned, but with a true and pure Heart, without all Hypocrisie; then your Redemption and Help will undoubtedly follow, so that in all Verity you will see and find the Winds and the Sea to obey you, and all Things to be brought to the desired End.

I wish man were but so disposed, as he would study to obtain somewhat with labour and Diligence, then certainly the Gods, the Presidents of Prosperity and Art would give Success, by which such a Disciple and Follower of Art might be assured, that in the wished School of Art, and desired Domicil of Grace, Felicity and Health should not be denied him, but that he himself should certainly see and find the Foundation of the Corner Stone, upon which he might commodiously build up all the other Orders of Stones. Then would cease the so many evilly founded Impertinencies of Bablers, which in the Schools stun the Ears of Disci-

ples,

ples, and in Houfes the Ears of the Sick; and the Matter it felf would fpeak, as it were with open Mouth, and by certain Experience confirm, that a Caftle or Palace of Stone cannot fo eafily be fet on Fire and burnt, as a Pidgeon-Houfe, or the old Neft of a Stork compofed of rotten Wood, and dayly dried more and more by the Sun.

But my Auditor and Difciple, do thou with fharp Judgment weigh this my fincere Information, and with fervent defire ftrive to penetrate the in-moft Center of Art, which by the external Face can be known by no man; profecute and prefs after the Virtue and Power thereof, no otherwife, than as a Hunter purfues a Wild Beaft; fearch out its Footfteps through the Snow, that you may rightly diftinguifh, and not take an Hart inftead of an Hind, or an Hare inftead of a Fox, or give a falfe eftimate thereof, by erring from its Foot-fteps. Well, caft out your Nets, and take a multitude of Fifhes, according to your own Wifh or Defire. Place your Threads as is behoofful, and difpofe of the Birds, which allure others to their place, and by this way of Fowling you will fulfil your defire with profit. That by thefe, to every Searcher I may briefly propofe my Admonition and Advice, I fay: My Friend the Hunter, difpofe rightly your Nets and Inftruments for Hunting as behoveth; and you Mariner, who Night and Day fayl through the vaft Seas, and are often driven hither and thither by the Winds, give heed to the Point of your Compafs, and undoubtedly you will reap profit, and not bring home your Ship, fwiftly returning, without great Gain of Merchandize.

But why do I treat of many things, or fpend time unprofitably (as tatling Sophifters are wont to do) in beating out the empty Chaff? I am de-ceived;

ceived ; I do not unprofitably spend my time;
for all the Words in my Writings are of use, and
in them are found few empty Letters, which contain not some Utility together with a profitable
Inftruction, fo that the time I spend in Writing
will rather be a Recreation, than a Burthen to me.
Therefore now, after the manner of Fencers, I will
ftep back one pace, and into the Chymical Labora-
tory infer a new Doctrine of External Things;
viz. fhew, that *Antimony* is of fuch a Nature, as
may be prepared fo, as to yield prefent help in Medicine pertinent to External Wounds, which ma-
nifoldly offer themfelves to us, and are declared
by Chirurgy. Therefore I will begin and briefly
explain my Proceffes, *viz.* how that is to be ufed
in Medicine , and how it may profitably be prepared.

Whofoever thou art, among Junior Students,
that defireft to fearch out the Occult things of Nature, and to bring her hidden Secrets to Light,
attend to what I fay, that thou mayeft be able to
diftinguifh Day from Night, and what is clear from
the Obfcure.

Take of *Hungarian Antimony* one part, Common
Salt half a part, and fix parts of *Argilla* not burnt,
grind all together , and diftil vehemently with a
continual Fire without Intermiffion and at length an
Oyl will come forth: from this abftract its Phlegm
by Diftillation, that a red dry Powder may remain
in the bottom of the *Cucurbit*. This Powder grind
fubtily, and refolve it into a Liquor, upon a Marble Stone; and you will have a red fhining Balfom
for Wounds, which far excels very many other
Balfoms. Its Ufe * is principally in Wounds ,
which have been a long time open , and in the
Cure of which the *Doctors* with their Plaifters ,
Unguents , Oyls and Ligaments could effect nothing;

thing : but with very great Difgrace they at length take off the Horfe's Bridle and Saddle, and return him to the Stable, whence they had him.

A wife General of an Army fo difpofeth his Souldiers in time of Fighting, that in the beginning of the Battle, the good and ftrong Souldiers fight, and in the End of the fame the beft and moft ftrong come to deal with the Enemy ; but fuch as are not powerful enough , for the firft and laft Encounter, in Arms or ftrength, are by him placed in the midft, that they may take Example of fighting from the Former, and hope of help and Victory from the Later. The Emperor is imitated by the Orator, in placing his Arguments fo , as he may overcome the minds of men. Bafilius imitates the Orator , in difpofing his Proceffes fo, as he may lead his Difciple to Sapience, and the Fruit of Wifdom. We have already had famous Proceffes, and in explaining them have ufed our Endeavour, and contributed fome Light. Now follow thofe, that are in themfelves clear enough, and not of fo great moment as the former ; therefore we fhall not infift upon them.

My Form of Speaking Savours of Simplicity ; for I am a man Religious, to whom the Method of Secular Men is unknown ; therefore cannot fo clearly detect and defcribe all Things, as the Matter it felf feems to require. Such a man as I, as to the Terms, becaufe he cannot fo formally ufe them, defires to be pardoned in this, and if he neglect any thing therein, he craves the candid Acceptation of all men, and in refpect of his State offers himfelf willing and ready to ferve all *Chriftians* Day and Night, and by his Prayers to *G O D*, to recompence this their Benevolence.

This Oyl is falutary in many grievous Accidents, and efpecially in old wounds, fo that few Medicines are found, which muft not give place to this. Only that Oyl, which is prepared with the Vulgar Sublimate of Apothecaries, is equal unto it in Effects, and is oftentimes by Experience found to be better, efpecially in the *Wolf* and *Cancer*, and in the *Noli me tangere*. But in ordinary Fiftula's, and the *Herpes* the fuperiour Oyl effects wonders, which were they not confirmed by Experience, could not be believed, and all which I recite not, left fome

one

one or other ſhould judge me to do it from Ambition, or that thence I hunt after Fame, which was
never by me either ſought or deſired ; nor at this
time, as I can holily affirm, is it aimed at by me.

Now I will give you the Preparation of another
Oyl.

Take *Mercury* mortified (which is ſublimed to
clearneſs and Splendor, and ſold by Apothecaries)
and *Antimony*, of each equal parts. Grind them
together, and diſtil them by ſuch a Retort, as will
retain the Spirits thrice , and afterward rectifie
this Oyl with Spirit of Wine. Then the Operation is abſolved, and the Oyl becomes red as Blood ;
but at firſt it is White, and like Ice or congealed
Butter. This Oyl effects wonders in many Affects,
where Nature gave no hope of Amendment, and
it always moſtly ſhews its force , virtue , power,
and efficacy, in the perfect Emendation of Evil into Good.

By Addition may be prepared another Oyl very profitable in external Wounds.

Take of *Antimony* one part , *Sulphur* one part,
Sal-Armoniack, or Salt of Urine purified half a
part, and *Calx-Vive* two parts. Expel the Oyl
ſtrongly : whatſoever is ſublimed, that grind with
the *Caput-mortuum*, and thereon again pour the
Oyl diſtilled off, and thrice diſtil it ; then the Oyl
is prepared.

When old Wounds can in no wiſe be healed,
then uſe this Oyl. For it is ſtrong, potent and penetrative: and lays a good Ground (even as Oyl of
Vitriol doth) for future Sanation.

An admirable Balſom of divers Ingredients (a-
mong which is *Antimony*) very uſeful in old
Wounds, is thus prepared.

Take of *Sulphur* ℥iiij. ſet it over a moderate
Fire to melt, and put into it half a pound of *Mer-*
cury,

cury, and ſtir the Mixture ſo long together, as until both become one Maſs. This Maſs grind to
Powder (for it is made as *Cinnabar* is wont to be
prepared) then grind with it ʒiiij. of *Antimony*, of
red *Arſenick* ʒiiij. of *Crocus Martis* ʒij. and of
Powder of Tiles ʒviij. Put all theſe into a Glaſs
Cucurbit, and ſublime them, as ſuch things are
wont to be ſublimed; and in this Sublimation you
will have Rubies in Colour not inferiour to the Ori-
ental, but they are not fixed; for they are volatile,
and fly from the Fire. Let the Artificer ſeparate
theſe Rubies from the Cinnabar, which aſcends in
the Sublimation, grind them to Powder and extract them with ſtrong Vinegar. This being done.
let him abſtract the Vinegar leaſurely in *B. M.* and
a Powder will remain; this Powder grind ſmall as
before, and having put it into another Glaſs, extract its Tincture with Spirit of Wine, and ſeparate the remaining Feces. This Extraction with
Spirit of Wine digeſt in *B. M.* well cloſed for one
Month. Then abſtract the Spirit of Wine, as
you abſtracted the Vinegar, and put the remaining, Powder of Wine into a flat Glaſs Diſh, and ſet
that Diſh in a Cellar into a Pail full of Water, that
it may Swim upon the Water, as a Boat. So doing. the Powder which is in the Glaſs will in a few
days reſolve it ſelf into a clear and perlucid Liquor.

    This Liquor is ſalutary in old open Wounds,
and is a vulnerary Balſom in like Accidents, if put
into them, and they covered round with a common
Stiptick Plaiſter. In diuturnal open Wounds, it
leaves no man deſtitute of help, although ſuch, as
in the Cure of which all other Remedies have been
tried in vain. Of open Ulcers, which have their
Original from within, I ſpeak not here; for they
cannot perfectly be healed without internal Remedies,

nedies, which drye up all Fluxions, and radically
extirpate the Difeafe: although at this time few
are found, who bend their thoughts this way, or
ake any Courfe to touch the Root it felf of thofe
Difeafes, of which I now treat.

If Men would in their Minds well confider the
Calamities of Life, into which the Fall of our firft
Parents precipited us, and ferioufly weigh that O-
riginal Sin, and the great troop of Evills thence
iffuing, *Viz*.: of Sadnefs, Anguifh, Difeafes and
Miferies, they certainly would fpend their time
better, and imploy more labour to fearch out the
health of their neighbours, fo ftrictly commended
to them by the Supream Ruler of Heaven, and by
him commanded as their proper Duty. But how
many (with grief be it fpoken!) fhunning labour,
confume their time unprofitably, and do not what
was to be done by them, but what they formerly
have done, and ftill have a luft to do, being affrayd
to do fo much, as will foyl their Fingers Ends; as
if they did envy the Tradefman, who perhaps gets
a fmall Gain by felling Soap, which they would not
willingly buy, to wafh their delicate hands. Are
not all we miferable Mortals, that live here, Stran-
gers in the Earth, poffeffing nothing, that we can
call ours? Are not all Things we here ufe, the
Goods of our *Lord*, lent to us, whilft we live and
no longer? Therefore we ought fo to behave our
Selves in ufing them, that fupported with a good
Confcience we may be able to ftand in that Day,
in which an Account is to be given for them; and
be not for our Ingratitude caft into Prifon, and ut-
ter Darknefs where fhall be weeping and gnafhing
of Teeth. If this were the Meditation, and this
the Intention of every Man, he would be like a
Monfter, if he fhould think of admitting Sin in himfelf, or of neglecting his Office; and all Men

would,

would, with a certain Emulation ftrive to pleafure their Neighbours, with the Gifts received from *GOD*. But thefe things are remote from the thoughts of the World, and Wordly Men; *Money, Money*, is the Scope of all their Intentions; this the Potent feek directly or indirectly, and for this the Poor are fubfervient to them, that they alfo may participate of the Mammon of Iniquity.

Yet take heed, I advife you to take heed, left the Bones of that Flefh, fticking in your Throat, Suffocate you, or the Back-bones of Fifhes pierce your Heart. But what doth Admonition help which the World little efteemes of and derides? Hear, I pray you an Hiftory; or learn a Parable. When I, according to my Vow, undertook a Pilgrimage to St. *James*, to vifit that holy Place as a Stranger, I prayed to *GOD*, and bound myfelf with a Vow, that if he granted me an happy Return to my Monaftery, I would render him due Prayers. He granted my Requeft, and I daily return Thanks to him. But I thought many more would have rejoyced with me, and have given thanks to the fame *GOD*, for the famous Reliques, which at that time I brought with me to our Monaftery, (for Confolation of the Poor, and many Others) that it might procure to it felf a Name, in this perifhing Valley of Tears, that could not bee wiped out by any Oblivion. Yet hence few were rendred either better, or more grateful to *GOD*, for fo great a benefit; but perfevered in Derifion and Contempt of that, which *GOD* will vindicate in the laft Day.

But of thefe enough at this time, let us proceed in our Inftruction of *Antimony*, whence yet another Medicine may be prepared, which I my felf have experienced to be very falutary; and effectual in every kind of Feavers, and in the Peftilence.

Grind

Grind *Antimony* fubtily, put it into a Glafs Re-
:ort, and diftil it with a ftrong fire, without any
Addition, 3. or 4. times, and alwayes with a large
Receiving Veffel; at length of it is made a Red
Pouder, which extract with Vinegar,and circulate
:he Extraction with a gentle fire for ten whole
Dayes; abftract the Vinegar by Diftilling, and that
which remains, by a fingular * Artifice in diftilling
will be changed into an Oyl. Let this Oyl be further Circulated until all Humidity be drawn off
therefrom, and it again be reduced to Pouder, as
:t was; when the Vinegar is abftracted and feparated by Diftillation, then gather the Oyl in a new
Receiver.

* *This Extraction may be rendred volatile with Spirit of Wine, after the fame
manner, as I taught you in the former Operations.*

Four Grains of this Oyl taken with water of *Car-
duus Benedictas*, if the Sick be well covered and
Sweated,heal *Quotidian, Tertian & Quartan* Fevers.
The fame Dofe is very available for expelling the
Peft, either given with Spirit of Wine, or with
diftilled Vinegar, according as the *Paroxyfm* of
the Peft firft invades, either with Heat, or with
Cold.Which is witneffed by three Brethren in our
Monaftery, who recovered of the Plague by this
Arcanum, when they expected no other but Death,
and had made their Wills. This fo reconciled
their Minds to this my Art, as they helped me,
with greater Zeal then before,both by their Prayers and Labour,and fpent the leifure time they had
exempt from Religious Dutyes, in ferving me dayly; and in a fhort time attained to fo great Experience, that by their own Induftry, and the Induftry of their Brethren, they gained more true
Knowledge in fearching out the Arcanums of Nature,

ture, then they could before obtain in a longer
series of time. Therefore, for these Men, I
give them thanks, even unto my very old Age;
and in very deed I return them thanks, because
they deserved so well of me, and of others, by their
so faithful Labour; but they finished their Course
of this Life before me, and entred the way of all
Flesh, wherefore I recommend their Reward to the
Supreme Physitian, who dwells in the higheft Heavens, and there will refresh them with sufficient
Joy, and make up in Heaven that Just Recompence,
which here on Earth was denyed them by ignorant,
and ungrateful Men.

Another Oyl of *Antimony* for wounds, is prepared with Addition in the following Manner.

Take of *Antimony*, *Sulphur*, *Saltnitre*, of each e-
qual parts; Fulminate those under a Bell, as Oyl of
Sulphur per Campan. is made; which way of preparing hath long since been known to the Antients.
But Confider, you will have a better way, if inftead
of a Bell, you take an Alembeck *, and apply to it
a Recipient; so you will obtain more Oyl, which
will indeed be of the same Colour, as that which is
made of Common Sulphur, but in powers and virtues not a little more excellent, then it.

---

* *I now, O Lover of Chymiftry, Speak to you by Pictures, not in words only
that by a Compendium of Speech, you may also have this Compendium of Labour,
and Charge.   Behold this Inftrument,*

Here place the Figure in page. 128.

and provide for your self such an One, that you may follow Basilius, *in making
Oyl of Sulphur* per Campan. *For this way* ʒj. *will yield you as much Oyl, a
a Pound will make in the Common Method. From Sixteen ounces of Sulphu
you may extract half an Ounce of Oyl, which others, in their way, do scarcely ex
pect from Sixteen pounds.*

W.

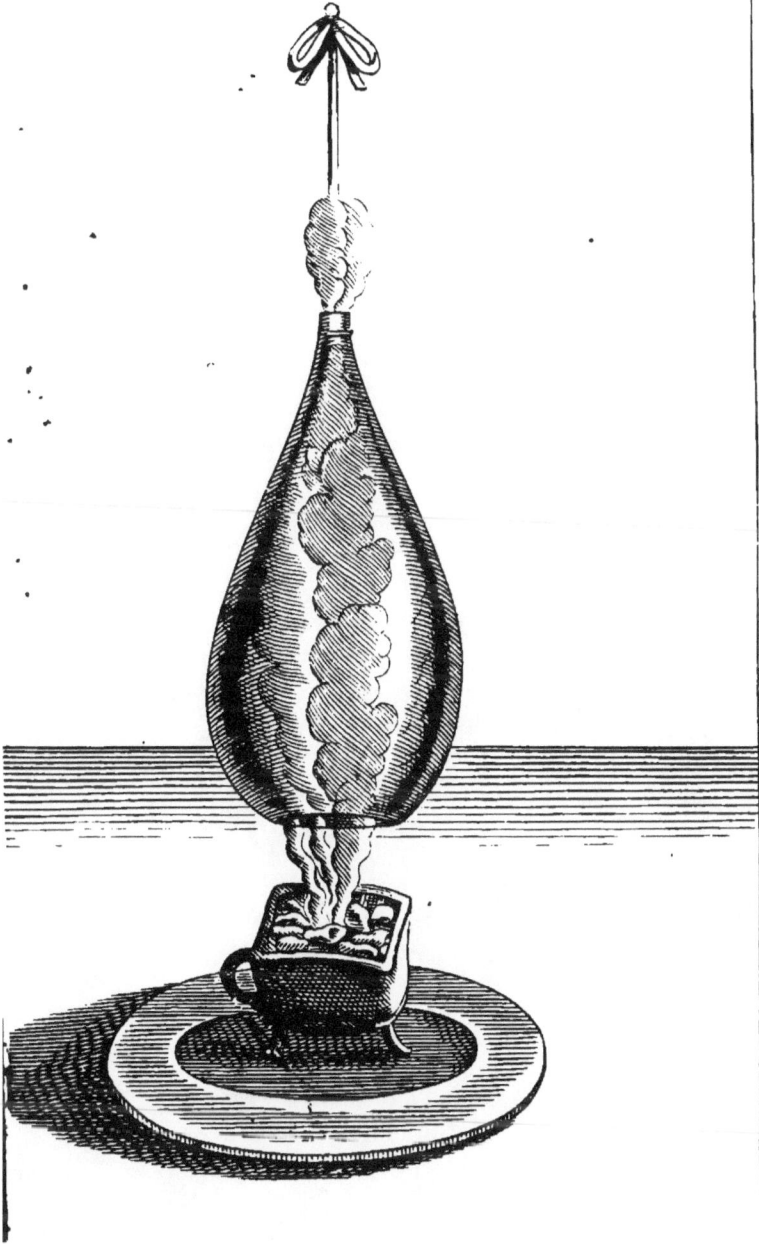

We use 3 or 4. Drops of this inwardly taken with Spirit of Wine against the Phthisick of the Lungs; but outwardly, if it first be anointed, and a Stiptick Playster applyed, against all Wounds stinking, and tending to putrefaction, and so will find it to be the most certain Remedy of all Wounds.

Again another Oyl of Antimony against all corroding Wounds very profitable, is this way made.

Take of *Antimony* ℔. j. Common Salt dryed, ℔. ß. Tiles broken; ℔. v. Grind all together, and put them into a Retort, whence distil a Yellow Oyl. When all the Spirits are come forth, put the Matter in another Glass. and from it extract the Plegm, and a Pouder will remain; which in an humid place spread upon a stone, and you will have an Humid Balsom, which is a singular Remedy in all Verminant Wounds, and in the Cancer, which hath being cheifly in the Face of a Man, and in the Breasts of a Woman. Much more might be written of this Balsom, did I not fear, that every unskillful Man, and the Rabble of Sophisters would fall foul on me, and say I speak too largely, and commit more to writing, then Experience hath taught me; and so that I boast only of Speculations, and mere Imaginations.

Moreover, another Oyl is made in this manner.

Sublime one part of *Antimony*, with a fourth part of Sal Armoniack, with subtile Fire. The Salt carryes up the Sulphur of *Antimony*, red as Blood. Grind this Sublimate to a fine Powder, and if you took at first ℔.j. of *Antimony*, grind with it again ℥v. of Sal Armoniack, and Sublime as before. The Sublimate dissolve in a moyst place. Or otherwise, take the Sublimate, and edulcorate it from the Salt added, gently dry it, and you will have Sulphur,

K which

which burns like Common Sulphur, which is ſold
at the Apothecaries. From this Sulpur extract
its Tincture with diſtilled Vinegar, and when you
have abſtracted the Vinegar by gentle Heat of
B. M. and by a ſubtile Operation again diſtilled
the remaining Pouder, you will have (if in this
Operation you erre not) a moſt Excellent * Oyl
grateful, Sweet, and pleaſant in its uſe, without
any Corroſiveneſs or peril.

* *This is another Repetition of the Proceſs, by which the Balſom of* Antimony
is made, as our Author calls it in this Treatiſe, or the Quinteſſence of Antimony,
of which often above. Yet in the proceſs there is this difference, that here the
Sulphur is ſeparated by the Sal Armoniack from the Antimony, *and then extracted*
from the Vinegar; whereas, in the other Proceſſe, the Sulphur is extracted by the
Vinegar, whilſt it is yet united with the Antimony. *But theſe are not things*
of ſo great a Moment, as to fruſtrate the Effect of Operations. Therefore this
Variety gives the greater Liberty to the Operator, that he may not be Scrupulous
in thoſe Things, in which he underſtands the Reaſon of what he doth, and of
the Method by which he acts.

It heals the Phthiſick, remedies the Priekings of
the Sides; and if any One labours with difficulty of
Breathing, let him take too Granes in the morning,
and as many at Night going to Bed. in the Elixir or
Spirit of Wine, and he ſhall be healed,   For it di-
lates the Paſſages of the Breaſt, expells all Impurities, and Phlegmes out of the Breaſt; and to me it
hath often produced many unlooked for Effects.
But ſince in other Preparations of *Antimony*, I have
deſcribed ſuch Virtues, as with this are common to
them, I Judge it needleſs to repeat them all, leſt
in the Sectators of Art I ſhould create tediouſneſs
through multiplicity of Words. or alien thoughts
by an impertinent Tautology.
In the mean while, the Liquor, which, as I above
ſaid, was reſolved in an Humid Place, is an external Medicine, and very profitable; for it cleanſeth
the

the Impurities of the Skin, and if a little Oyl of Tartar be mixed therewith, it heals the Phagedena of the Fingers ; and if often anointed therewith, it purifyes the Skin and cures Scrophulaes.

Also, Sulphur of *Antimony* is prepared in another Manner.

Grind *Antimony* to a fine Pouder, which boyl for two hours or a little longer, in a sharp Lixivium made of the Ashes of Beech-wood. When boyled, filter the *Antimony* clear, and poor Vinegar upon the filtred Liquor, and then the Sulphur will settle to the bottom wholly red. Pour off the Phlegm and gently dry the Pouder. Distil this Pouder with the Vinegar of Wine ; extract the Tincture, and do as you did with the former Sulphur. .. To reduce the same into an Oyl by Distiling, is worth your while : Although the Oyl above mentioned hath greater Virtues, because its Body, by the Sal Armoniack, in the beginning of the Sublimation was better dissolved and opened.

There yet remain many things to be written of *Antimony*, and especially Three, necessary to be known by the *Spagyrick* Physitian and Philosopher, *viz.* the Preparation of Vinegar, which is made of its Minera; and then the Philosophick Signate Star, which is not to be omitted; and lastly the Lead of Philosophers, of which we shall speak somewhat; touching which Many have imagined Great Things, and thought (in their way of Reasoning, and Speculation) to prepare the true and syncere Mercury of Philosophers of it; which indeed cannot be done, since so great Efficacy is not from above infited in *Antimony*, as that in it can exist that Mercury, or of it be prepared. That Mercury is the first *Ens*, or first Water of Metalls, which is perfect, otherwise the Great Stone of the ancient Wise Men could not be made of it. That first

Ens, I ſay, and the Seeds thereof, are found in another Mineral, in which the Operation (according to the Genius of Metalls) is greater, then in *Antimony.* Yet this ſupplyes us with a certain Particular, and moſt profitable Operation ; and beſides in it you may find whatſoever appertains to internal and external Medicine. For it is the *Column* of ever Shop of Apothecaries, if duely prepared, as I often admoniſh ; nor is any thing wanting in it, provided the Artiſt hath learned well to diſtinguiſh the Diſpoſition of Metalls and Mineralls, and diligently obſerves both the Preparation and Uſe of *Antimony*; becauſe then, and not before, follows a perfect Judgement of it. Therefore I will ſtand to my Promiſe, and comfort my Diſciples, according to their Wiſh, by ſatisfying and inſtructing them, which way the Separation of Good from Evil may be known to them, and giving Information touching the Vinegar of Philoſophers, which is made of *Antimony.*

Melt the Minera of *Antimony,* and purify it, grind it to a Subtile Pouder, this Matter put into a Round Glaſs, which is called a Phiall, having a long Neck, pour upon it diſtilled Water, that the Veſſel may be half full. Then having well cloſed the Veſſel, ſet it to putrefy in Horſedung, until the Minera begin to wax hot, and caſt out a Froath to the Superficies: then 'tis time to take it out ; for that is a Sign the Body is opened. This digeſted Matter put into a Cucurbit, which well cloſe, and extract the Water, which will have an acid Taſte. When all the Water is come off, intend the Fire, and a Sublimate will aſcend ; this again grinde with the *Feces,* and again pour on the ſame Water, and a ſecond time abſtract it, then it will be more Sharp. This Operation muſt be repeated, until the Water be made as Acid, as any other Sharp, diſtilled,

diſtilled Vinegar of Wine. But the Sublimate, the oftner the Operation is repeated, the more it is diminiſhed. When you have obtained this Acid Vinegar, take freſh Minera as before and pour this Vinegar on it, ſo as it may ſtand above it three Fingers; put it into a Pelican, and digeſt it two dayes in Heat, then the Vinegar becomes red, and much more ſharp then before. Cant this clean off, and diſtil it without Addition in *B. M.* The Vinegar comes off white, and the Redneſs remains in the Bottom, which extracted with Spirit of Wine is an excellent Medicine. Again rectify the Vinegar in *B. M.* that it may be freed from its Phlegm; laſtly diſſolve in it its proper Salt, *viz :* in ℥iiij. of it, ℥j. of the Salt, and force it ſtrongly by Aſhes; then the * Vinegar becomes more ſharp, and acquires greater Strength, and virtue.

---

* *This Vinegar alſo is numbred among the chief of thoſe things, which are prepared of* Antimony, *therefore I thought it worth while to illuſtrate this with ſome Commentaries. For although it may be made in the way* Baſilius *preſcribes, yet there are ſtill ſome things wanting to render the work both more eaſy and more perfect, which I here ſubjoyn; For ſix pounds of* Antimony *are required ſixteen pounds of Diſtilled Water, and when (after Digeſtion) we would diſtil it , a certain manual Operation muſt be obſerved, on which depends the Succeſs of the whole work almoſt. For the Alembeck muſt be ſo placed, as his Pipe or Beak may be covered with Water, which either muſt be put into the Recipient, or paſs out by diſtilling into the ſame; otherwiſe the Spirit's of the Antimony will be loſt, and more then half part of the ſame periſh, or the work require much more time for its perfection. I have expreſſed this by a Figure here placed, that if*

Here place the Figure in the 133. Page.

any by hearing do not ſufficiently perceive this, they may by ſeeing underſtand. When the whole Water hath paſſed over by Alembeck the Fire (as the Author admoniſheth) is to be increaſed, and three Dayes, and as many Nights continued without intermiſſion. Then let all cool, and the Sublimate, as he teaches, muſt as

K 2 Thiſ

gain be mixed with the Antimony; this Labour for three Days and Nights must be re-assumed, and afterward repeated to the third time. Then your Water will be acid, as common Vinegar. If you tinge this Vinegar with new Minera of Antimony, you will have a Tincture, which Basilius names his Balsome of Life, so often described, but never sufficiently commended. O, did Mortals know what Mysteries lye absconded in this Tincture, I question whether they would be desirous to set about any other Preparation of Antimony. All things are in this One. I have spoken, O Lover of Chymistry, do thou act.

This Vinegar Cools vehemently, not as common Vinegar, but with great Admiration, and certain Experience, especially for assuaging the Gangræne, produced from Gunpowder; also it heals other enraged Wounds and Members, when joyned with the Soul of Saturn, wrought up into an Unguent, and applyed outwardly. And mixt with Water of Endive, to which Salt prunell: is added, it consumes the Squinancy, and extinguisheth its great Heat: besides, it assuageth the Motion of the Blond inflamed. In time of the Pestilence, taken inwardly, the Dose of one Spoonful, several times, and outwardly applyed to the Swellings by Linen Clothes moystned therein, extracts the Venom, and most excellently cools: But consider, when you would use it in this manner outwardly, it must be mixed with a third part of Water distilled from Frogspawn.

Many highly esteem the Signate Star of Antimony, and very many have endeavoured to prepare it, sparing no labour to attain the same. Which some have acquired with good success, others have lost all their labour and Cost, Many have assumed an Opinion, that this Star is the true Matter, whence the Stone of Philosophers may be made, induced hereunto, by this thought or Imagination, viz. because Nature her self hath signed it into a Star, therefore they could not choose but esteem of it, and by these Cogitations were led into the Way of of Error, But I fyncerely denounce, that it is nothing fo. For thefe kind of Searchers erre from the Kings high-way, and kill themfelves in clambering up Rocks and Cliffs, in which wild Goats inhabit, and Birds of Prey build their nefts. It is not given to this Star to contain in it felf fo great Potency, or from it felf to form fo pretious a Stone. Yet I affirm, that in it lyes *abfconded* a famous Medicine, which may be made of it. The Star is thus made.

Take of *Hungarian Antimony* 3. parts. Of Steel 1. part. melt thefe together with 4. parts of burnt *Tartar*, when melted pour out the whole into a Cone, when cold take out the Regulus, and feparate it from all impurity, and the Scoria. Grinde this Regulus to Pouder and weigh it, then add thereto thrice fo much of burnt *Tartar*, and pour it out as before. Repeat this labour the third time; then the Regulus purgeth it felf, and becomes pure and clear. Note, when you have rightly compleated the Fufion, and have ufed a manual Operation, as is fit (which is of principal concern in this Work) you will obtain a fair Star * bright and fhining like Cupellate Silver, no lefs artificially formed, then if fome Painter had with his Compaffes diligently divided the fame.

* *Here it is to be noted. In the third fufion of the Regulus, the Fire muft be vehemently heightned, that if any Impurity remain with the Regulus, it may by that intenfe heat be taken away. By this means you will have a Regulus in beauty and whitenefs comparable to Silver, but in Virtue and Price far Superior.*

This Star with Sal Armoniack is reduced to a red * Sublimate; for the Tincture of *Mars* afcends. Such a Sublimate may be refolved in a moift place into a Liquor, which difcovers wonderful Virtues in Chirurgy.

This

* This Sublimate, before it is ſet in a Cellar to be there reſolved, ſhould be purged from the Sal Armoniack with diſtilled water. They are few Things which I admoniſh, but by the ignorance of theſe or thoſe, great Errors are committed, and the Work with all its Coſts and Charges periſheth, or at leaſt yeilds not ſufficient to pay what the Materials coſt.

This Regulus, or Signate Star, melted often with the Stony *Serpent*, is brought to ſuch a ſtate, as at length it conſumes it ſelf in it, and wholy unites it ſelf with the Serpent. * This being done, the *Sectator* of Art hath a Matter altogether hot and fiery in which very much of Art is *Latent*. This prepared Matter reſolves it ſelf into an Oyl; this very Oyl ought to be brought over the Helm by Diſtillation, and then rectifyed, that it may be pure and clear,

* Of a Snake or Serpent the Nature is ſuch, if you ſlacken your hold he riſeth up, if you gripe him hard he burſts, the ſame I ſear here: Therefore the Author calls that a Serpent, which he mixeth with this Regulus. But it is the Serpent of a Stone, or a Stony-Serpent; becauſe the Salt, as a Snake willingly licks a Stone.

This Oyl may commodiouſly and ſecurely be taken inwardly; but with great Prudence and Caution, and not oftner then twice or thrice in a Week, and no more at one time, then three Drops in ℥ij. of Wine, or other Water diſtilled from Herbs, according to the Exigency of the Diſeaſe. For this Reaſon, it is the Phyſitians part to know the Cauſes of Diſeaſes, together with the Complexion of the Sick, that he may the more ſecurely uſe his Remedies.

This is a famous *Acrimony* * containing in it ſelf many *Arcanums*; but there is no need to reveal all things together and at once to unskillful men. Some Arts are to be ſuppreſſed, that ſome Secrets and *Arcanums* may remain proper to the Philoſo-pher,

pher, who in searching them out hath daily
sustained grievous Toyl.

＊ *They, who understand of how great utility it is to extract the Essences from
Metals, are not ignorant of the Virtues of this sharp Oyl. For this is the only
Menstruum for this purpose. How many are they who have spent their whole
Life in Chymical Operations, and never could arrive to the knowledge of a
true Menstruum? To thee it is here revealed, if Health be your aim, you may
safely use it in the Body; if you attempt somewhat more sublime, and have
already conceived good hope you shall compound it, this is the principal help of
all, for ascending to the Throne of the Chymical Kingdom.*

But let him, who refolves to tread in my Foot-
steps not be weary of Searching; but what I
have done, let him do, and what I have fo often
defired, and what with fo earneft Wifhes I have
fought, let him feek. Thefe Principles, which I
have prefcribed you, are fufficient for to
fearch out the End by. Many have failed, yea
many have been cut off by Death, before they
could in their Learning attain to the Principles
only; that is, they were deprived of Life, before they could acquire the Magiftery of Art.
Therefore, I at firft fet forth a Book of Rudi-
ments, that the Studious follower of Art (who
in his firft Experiences had need of fo much time)
might the fooner attain his defired end, and
wifhed Scope, and next unto *GOD* give me
thanks.

Moreover, in this Oyl a wonderful Effect is
latent. For if this Oyl be circulated with Cryftals for fome time, *viz.* for three Days and
Nights (the Cryftals being firft Calcined) it from
them extracts a Salt: which being done, the Oyl
may again be diftilled off by Retort. Thus you
will have a Medicine, which admirably breaks
the Stone in the Bladder, and expels it; and alfo
effects

effects many other Things, by a certain famous virtue in it.

But that we may alfo fay fomething of the Lead
of Philofophers, let the curious fearchers of Nature know, that between *Antimony* and common
Lead, there is a certain near affinity, and they
hold a ſtrict friendſhip each with other. As a
Tree caſts out of it's ſide it's fuperfluous Roſin,
which is the Sulphur of that Tree; as the Cherry-
tree, and other Trees, which give forth ſuch
Gums: there are other kinds of Trees alfo, which
by reafon of their abundance of *Mercury*, produce
and caſt forth from themfelves a certain Excrefcen-
cy, which neither in Form, nor Virtue is in any
wife like to their Fruit; but hath wholy other
properties, as in Oaks and Apple-trees is apparent,
which produce like baſtard Fruits, or Monſters:
So the Earth alfo hath like abortive Fruits, which
in Separation from the pure Metals, are fevered and
caſt out.

Now, although there is fo ſtrict an affinity between *Antimony*, and *Saturn*; yet by reafon of the
too much *Sulphur*, which *Antimony* hath in it
felf, it is caſt out from it: becaufe its viſcous
Body (in it's Nativity) could not come to perfection; and therefore it was conſtrained neceſſarily to confiſt among Minerals: becaufe it's abundance of hot *Sulphur* was the Caufe, that hindred
it's *Mercury*, that through defect of Cold it could
neither come to Coagulation, nor into a Malleable
Body. Moreover, I fay, the Lead in *Antimony* is
no other, then it's Regulus, which hath not as yet
obtained Malleablenefs. And, as above I faid,
when the Regulus and Steel by Liquefaction are united, and deduced to a Star, there are many, who
would thence make the antient ſtone of Philofophers; which I before denyed to be poſſible. Yet
what

what Medicines may be prepared of it, you have already briefly heard; therefore touching them, I shall not add a Word more.

But the Reason, why the Regulus is called and accounted Lead, is this. When that Regulus is taken, which *Antimony* gives forth from it self in making Glafs, and put into a Crucible well clofed, which can refist the fire, with the Salt of *Saturn* (having been firft Cemented with the Salt for three hours) and thefe permitted to melt together, in a Wind Fornace, the * Regulus, when taken out, is found to be rendred foft, and more ponderous, then it was before. For it receives it's ponderofity from the Spirit of the Salt, which alfo gave it foftnefs, fo that it's Body now is compact and heavy.

---

* *I not envioufly, as many Chymifts do, but affectionately deal with Chirurgeons: wifhing that they would in their mind, as according to their faculty they may and ought, endeavor to prepare fuch helps, for their miferably afflicted Patients, and fuch Compendiums of Sanity, as may be prepared of this* Regulus. *Would you, have me difcover to you the Myftery? Hear with pleafure, and ufe it. This* Regulus, *by the* Salt *of* Saturn *rendred* Malleable, *muft be mixed with equal parts of* Mercury *condenfed by* Saturn, *and in a vehement fire fluxed, and fo well mixed. The Matter comes forth, in it's external Face like unto Silver, but in its internal Virtues is more noble, and more pretious then any* Silver. *But you Chyrurgeon, ftudious of your own Art, and by Art covetous of Glory, deduce that into thin Plates, and externally apply it to Wounds, and Malignane Fiftula's. So doing, you will be amazed, when you fhall fee Nature, helped by this Art, to perform more, in a very fhort time, then you could have hoped for in a longer time, by fo many Unguents and Plaifters. The Rufticks (to ufe the words of Bafilius) will no more deride and upbraid you, faying, they can effect more with a piece of crude and ftinking Lard, then you are able to do with the laborious Procefs of your whole Chirurgick Art.*

Therefore I fay, there is not much difference between the Signate Star, and Lead of *Antimony*; which notwithftanding are every where diftinguifhed as two divers things. For either of them is made of the Glafs of *Antimony*, and prepared into one and the ſame Medicine, as is already by me ſufficiently declared. Here therefore I break off my Diſcourſe, that I may explain what the ſtone of fire is, after I ſhall have declared the Appendix which follows.

O *GO D grant thy Grace, and open the Hearts and Ears of Men unwilling to hear, and to them impart thy Bleſſing, that they may acknowledge Thee in thy Omnipotency, and wonderful Works of Nature, to thy Praiſe, Honor and Glory, and for the Health, So-lace, and Confirmation of the Strength of their Neighbor, and alſo for Reſtoring the Sick to their priſtine Health.* Amen.

THE
APPENDIX.

FOr a Concluſion you are further to know, that *Antimony* may be applyed to many other Uſes, then as above expreſſed ; as to Scripture or Printing, for which Printers uſe it. Alſo under a certain Conſtellation and Concourſe of the Planets, a Mixture of Metals is made with *Antimony*, of which Artiſts form Signatures and Characters endued with ſingular Virtues. Of the ſame Mixture alſo are made Speculums, of many and wonderful Aſpects and Properties. Alſo Bells and other Inſtruments may be made thereof, of admirable ſound. Likewiſe Images of Men, and many other Things *.

But

* *The Virtues and powers of* Antimony *which the Author here in this Appendix so lightly toucheth, and passeth over, are so many and so various, as indeed the hundredth part of them is not yet known to Men. Which Ignorance undoubtedly redounds to the Reproach and Ignominy of our kind; because we Men, among so many other Animals, only endued with Reason, and a Faculty of Discoursing, are hurryed with so great impetuousness, to that wicked and abominable Desire of Gain, as scarcely any Man hath leisure to search out the wonders, which the Author of Nature hath insited in his Creatures. But I am unwilling to repeat this Reprehension so often spoken of by* Valentine *; I do only call it to mind. This Mineral, in which lies hid so admirable a Spirit, that by Exhausting it cannot be exhausted, hath also Virtues, which by no man studying can be sufficiently known. What I have tryed, out of the way of Chymistry and Medicine, are few ; yet Experience hath taught me so much, as I judge* Antimony *in other things will shew it self no less admirable, then in Chymistry and Medicine.*

Yet what I think of Characters and Signatures, which the Author saith may be made under a Concourse of certain Constellations, I shall not here discover. It sufficeth me, that I can say, that among all Metals and Minerals, there is not any Substance known, which contains so much of a Cœlestial Spirit, and hath so great Sympathy with the Stars, as Antimony. *Weigh this, with all that I have before said of* Antimony, *but not negligently, and Hasten to the* Stone, *which is called the* Stone of Fire.

But since thefe things concern not Medicine, nor appertain to my Order, Rule, and Calling, I reft well fatisfied in my Vocation, and commend them to the Handling of Others, who know them better.

O F

OF THE

Triumphant Chariot

OF

ANTIMONY,

AND

What the STONE of FIRE is.

Hen, at a certain time an abundance of Thoughts (which my
internal and fervent Prayer to
GOD fuggefted) had fet me
loofe and wholy free from all terrene Bufineffes, I
purpofed in my felf to attend to Spiritual Infpirati-
ons, of which we have need, for the more accurate fcrutiny of Nature. Therefore I refolved to
make my felf Wings, that I might afcend on high,
and infpect the ftars * themfelves, as *Icarus*, and
his Father *Dædalus* in times paft did, if credit
may be given to the Ancient Writings of Poets.

---

* *This Leave is to be given to all, who treat of Sacred Things, Viz. to declare
thofe Things, which they are willing to difcover (not to the unlearned ignorant Deriders, but only to Men, worthy, and to fuch as fincerely defire, and*

But

aspire to the knowledge of the same) in a certain singular and Parabolical kind of Writing. In which our Author is the more to be excused, because when he comes to the greatest of Mysteries, which he intended to explain in this Book, he betakes himself to certain hiding Places of Parables, and with the Heaven of Piety, which is wont to cover all things (yea even the most wicked) he so veils his Secrets, as None but Pious and sincere Disciples of Art can with the acuteness of their sight penetrate these Clouds. Do thou therefore,

Dum fugit ad Salices, & fe cupit ante videri,

with a certain intellectual Luxury sport with him, he will not delude Thee.

But when I foared too near the Sun, my Feathers with it's vehement heat were confumed, and burnt, I fell headlong into the depth of the Sea: yet to me, in this my extream Neceffity invoking *G O D*, help was fent from Heaven, which freed me from all peril and the prefent Deftruction. For an Angel haftned to my affiftance, who commanded the Waters they fhould be ftill, and inftantly, in that deep Abyfs appeared a moft high Mountain, upon which at length I afcended, that I might thereon examine, whether (as Men had affirmed) there was any Friendfhip * and Familiarity between Superiors and Inferiors, and whether the Superior Stars have acquired power from *G O D*, their Creator, to produce any one Thing like themfelves in the Earth.

* *There hath been no Man, who had darted his fight but as it were through a Lattice, into the Penetrals of Chymiftry, who did ever deny this Influence of Superiors upon Inferiors. Therefore let Bafilius fo holily affirming, and fo often openly declaring it to Men, be credited by thofe, who, the true Light being not yet rifen upon them, do by feeling without fight practice Chymiftry.*

And having fearched into Things, I found, that whatfoever the Ancient Mafters had fo many Ages fince committed to Writing, and delivered to their Difciples, who earneftly defired to be the true Imitators

Imitators of them, was (as I may say) more true than Truth it self. Wherefore, as is fit, I give prayse and thanks to my *Lord* and Heavenly Father, for his incomprehensible Works.

In very deed (that I may expound the matter in few Words) I found all Things, which are generated in the Bowels of Mountains, to be infused from the Superior Stars, and take their beginning from them, in the form of an *aqueous* Cloud, Fume or Vapour, which for a very long time fed and nourished by the Stars, is at length educted to a tangible form by the Elements. Moreover, this Vapor is dryed, that the Watrinefs may lofe its Dominion, and the Fire next, by help of the Air, retain the Ruling Power. Of Water Fire, and of Fire and Air Earth is produced: which notwithstanding are found in all things confifting of Body, before the Separation of them. Therefore this, *viz*. Water is the firft Matter * of all things, which by the Drynefs of Fire and Air is formed into Earth.

* *This is an old Song, this is the Sum of Art ; from this Imitation of Nature is found the leffer Stone of Fire, from this it is made, whenfoever it is prepared, from the Same alfo the great Philofophick Stone derives its Original. This is the Water of* Anaxagoras, *the Fire of* Empedocles, *and* Ariftotle's *firft Matter, of which all things have been, and to this Day are made. Which is clearly evident in the Nutrition of Man, the Growth of a Tree, and in the Generation of Metalls, For that, which conftitutes Flefh, Woods, and Metalls, is not taken from Food, Rain or Earth, but is infufed into them from elfwhere. That very Thing is the Aliment, which nourifheth all things, but that it may be fo varioufly fpecificate, it muft be feparated from that Body, in which it dwells, and be joyned to another, which by the Chymical Art is performed.*

But now fince my Intention is to defcribe the Stone of Fire, how it is made of *Antimony*, together with the Procefs of its Preparation, which not only heals Men, but Metalls alfo particularly; it will be neceffary before all Things, to fpeak fome-

L what

what of thefe following Heads. What properly
the Stone of Fire is; what is its Minera; whether
a Stone can be made without Matter or no; what
is the extreme difference of Stones, and how many
Species of them are found, and laftly of their ufe.

*In this my purpofe, I pray, O Spirit of Heaven
illuminate me, that I may give a true and fyncere
Inftruction,* viz. *according as is fit for me, and
the matter it felf permits. Indeed I have hopes of
Eternal Abfolution from this my Supream confef-
for, who from Eternity poffeffeth the Throne of
Mercy, and will give Teftimony of all Things,
when the Decretory Sentence fhall be pronounced
upon all Men, in the laft Judgement, without any
appeal.*

Therefore firft know and confider, that the
True Tincture of *Antimony,* which is the Medicine
of Men and Metalls, is not made of crude and melted *Antimony,* as it is fold by Merchants and Apothecaries; but extracted from the Minera, as it is
taken out of the Mountains, and before it is formed into Glafs. But how that Extraction fhould
be made, is the principal Work in which the whole
Art confifts : Health and Riches attend him, who
rightly attains to that. But, my Reader, you muft
diligently mind this, *viz.* that the Tincture of
Antimony prepared, fixed and folid, or the Stone of
Fire (as I name it) is a certain pure, penetrative
fpiritual and fiery Effence, which is reduced into a
coagulated Matter, like the Salamander, which in
Fire is not confumed, but purified and confer-
ved.

Yet the Stone of Fire tingeth not univerfally, as
the Stone * of Philofophers, which is made of the
Effence of Gold it felf. To this no fuch power is
given, as that it fhould perform fuch things, but it
tingeth particularly; *viz,* Silver into Gold, Tin
alfo

also and Lead; but *Mars* and *Venus* it toucheth not, nor do they yield more, then from them by Separation may be effected.

* As much as Heaven is elevated above the Earth, so much doth the true Stone of Philosophers differ from this Stone of Fire. I my self do candidly confess, that although I have found this, yet I am very far distant from the other. And this, whatsoever it is, I own to be received from the wisdome of Basilius. Do you take heed you be not deluded by your own phantasie, and that others deceive you not.

Moreover, one part of it can tinge no more, then five parts of Metall, so as to persist in the Tryal of *Saturn* and *Antimony*; whereas, on the contrary, the Great Stone of Philosophers can transmute to infinity. Also in augmentation it cannot be so far exalted; yet the Gold is pure and solid.

The Minera, out of which this Stone or Tincture is made, is no other then (as I above mentioned) the very Earth of *Antimony*; from which, I say, it is made: but how or with what virtue, force, and power it is endued, you shall hear anon.

Let the Reader consider, that there are many kinds of Stones found, which tinge particularly; but all fixed Pouders, which tinge, I here signify by the name of Stones; yet one tingeth more highly then another, as especially the Stone of Philosophers, which obtains the principal place; the next is the Tincture of *Sol*; and of *Luna*, &c. For the White: after these, the Tincture of *Vitriol* or *Venus*; likewise the Tincture of *Mars*; either of which hath in it self the Tincture of *Sol*, when reduced to Fixation. Next to these follow the Tinctures of *Jupiter* and *Saturn* for Coagulation of *Mercury*; and lastly, the Tincture of *Mercury* it self. This is the difference and multiplicity of Stones and Tinctures, all which notwithstanding

are

are generated from Seed, and from one original *Matrix*, from which the true Univerſal Stone proceeds, but out of theſe no other Metallick Tincture is to be found. But all other Things, by what name foever called, all Stones (whether pretious or common) I touch not now, nor have I any Intention to write or ſpeak any thing of them at this time; becauſe they contain in themſelves no other Virtues, then what appertain to Medicine. Nor ſhall I here make mention of *Animal* or *Vegetable* Stones; becauſe they are only conducent to Medicine; but for Metallick Works unprofitable and voyd of all Virtue. Yet all the Virtues of all Things, *Mineral*, *Animal* and *Vegetable*, collected into one, are found in the Stone of Philoſophers.

Salts are endued with no tinging Virtue, but are onely Keys * for the Preparation of Stones; otherwiſe of themſelves they effect nothing.

* *Salts, as here is rightly ſaid, are Keyes; they open the Cheſt wherein the Treaſure lyes. But you muſt be ſure to take the true Key; otherwiſe you may ſpoyl the Lock, and not open the Cheſt. It is not ſafe in this Caſe to take Quid for Quo, as Apothecaries are wont. You muſt have a Philoſophick Key, and proper Salts fit for opening muſt be taken. Nor contemn that Diſtinction, which is intimated, between Salts opening, which the Author here calls (as they are) Keys, and Salts fixing, which enter the Treaſure it ſelf; as is ſufficiently manifeſt by the Text.*

Yet, as for Metallick Salts (I now ſpeak to the purpoſe if you rightly underſtand, what diſtinction I put between Mineral Salts) they are not to be ſlightly eſteemed, nor to be rejected in Tinctures, ſince we can in no wiſe be without them, in their Compoſition, For in them lyes that moſt pretious Treaſure, from which every Fixation derives its Original.

Here ſome may ask, and indeed very properly; whether ſuch a Stone can be made without matter?

J

I anſwer, No. For every Thing muſt have its own Matter; but not without Diſtinction. *Animals* require their Matter, *Vegetables* theirs, and *Mineralls* theirs. Only conſider and before all things obſerve this; *viz.* that no Body can be profitable for any Stone, without Fermentation, which I find in the end of the Work (I mean as to the Preparation of the Great Stone) cannot be omitted, if I would convert Metalls with gain ; for although in the Beginning a Corporal form, and corporal Entity, viſible and tangible is taken ; yet from that formal Body muſt be extracted a certain Spiritual and Celeſtial Entity (ſhall I call it) or Apparency ; for I find no other more fit name to give it: which Entity was by the Stars, before infuſed into that Body, and by the Elements concocted and made perfect. Yet this Spiritual Entity muſt again by a leſſer Fire, and by the *Regimen* and Direction of the Microcoſm, be reduced to a tangible, fixed, Solid and inconſumptible Matter.

But what do I, or what do I ſpeak? I act as if I were deprived of my Reaſon, * in uttering words ſo openly. For if I had either Reaſon or Judgement, I ſhould not diſcover ſo great Things with my Tongue, or command my hand to proceed in writing them.

* *Art thou well in thy Wits,* Baſilius, *who doeſt thus proſtitude the* Arcanum *of the Stone, which hath unto this day been ſo diligently abſconded by all Philoſophers? Surely, if thou hadſt not laboured with I know not what Intemperance of Mind, thou wouldeſt have cloſed thy Lips, and not have ſo clearly opened, what it is is to ſeparate the Pure from the Impure, what to render the fixed volatile, and again to fix that; how the Inferior becomes Superior, and that again plunged into the Deep Abyſſe, from which it had aſcended. To diſcover ſo many Myſteries, in ſo few Words, as here thou doeſt, aſſuredly if it be not Madneſs, it is a certain very great benevolence to Poſterity. This is that which moved him.* Valentine *ſeems to have burned with this Affection, and could not overcome*

that Inclination of Well-doing to many, by the Obligation (impoſed on all Philo-
ſophers) of concealing that Secret Myſtery of Nature, which by the Author there-
of, that is, by Nature naturating with Intellectual Revelation, is communicated
only to the Sons of Art worthy and choſen. The Secret of Secrets hath fallen from
Baſilius, *do thou Reader attend, if you find the* Pearl, *be not like* Æſop's
Cock.

All Tinctures of Metalls ought to be ſeparated,
as that they may be moved with a certain principal Love and Affection to Metalls, and have a pro-
penſity and deſire of uniting themſelves with them,
and of reducing them to a better State. Will
you have an Emblem, or Example? Behold here it
is of Man and Woman. If they two be inflamed
with Mutual Love, neither Delay, nor Reſt is admitted, until they be united, and their Deſire is ſa-
tisfyed : after this Union they reſt, and are multiplyed, according to the good pleaſure of *G O D,*
and the promiſe of his Bleſſing.

Man lives obnoxious to many and perillous
Diſeaſes, ſome of which debilitate and conſume the
powers of Nature ſo, as the Man can by no Reme-
diesbe perfectly reſtored to Health and his former
Strength. But Love is a diſeaſe, with which no
other Diſeaſe may be compared, which is not healed unleſs by Production of its own like, which either Sex deſireth, and that Deſire is not ſatisfied,
unleſs by fulfilling this will of the enkindled affection. How many Teſtimonies of this violence,
which is in Love, are daily found? for it not only
inflames the Younger Sort, but it ſo exagitates
ſome Perſons far gon in years, as through the burning Heat thereof, they are almoſt mad. Natural Diſeaſes are for the moſt part governed by the
Complexion of Man, and therefore invade ſome
more fiercely, others more gently; but Love,
without diſtinction of poor or rich, young or old,
ſiezeth All, and having ſeized ſo blinds them, as
for-

forgetting all Rules of Reafon, they neither fee or
fear any Snare. Peculiar Members are infected
with the Singular Symptomes of other Difeafes,
all the other parts remaining found and free from
that Dolour. Whom Love infects, it invades all
over, penetrates the Body and its whole Subftance,
Form, and Effence, and leaves nothing unoffended.
For taking place in the Heart there it kindles a
Fire, the burning heat of which is diffufed through
the Veins, Arteries, and all the Members of the
Body, and in a word I fay, where Love once hath
fixed its Root, the man is fo deprived of all fenfe,
reafon and underftanding, as he forgets all things,
ferioufly minds nothing ; he is unmindful of
G O D and his Law, his promifes and threats he little regards ; the torments of Hell and rewards of
Eternal Life he contemns. I fpeak of inordinate
and unlawful Love, to which, if a man be once addicted, he adheres fo pertinacioufly, as nothing
can reclaim, nothing can reftrain him; he forgets
his Duty, Calling and Condition ; derides all admonition, defpifeth the Counfels of Parents, Superiors, and others who wifh him well ; briefly I fay,
he is fo blind with Love, as he cannot fee his own
Mifery ; fo deaf, as he cannot hear thofe, who by
their faithful Advice, endeavour to turn and avert
from him, the dammage and evil, which would be-
fall him. Love leaves nothing intire, or found in
the Man ; it impedes his Sleep, he cannot reft either Night or Day ; it takes off his Appetite, that
he hath no difpofition either to Meat or Drink, by
reafon of the continual Torments of his Heart and
Mind. It deprives him of all Providence ; hence
he neglects his Affairs, Vocation, and Bufinefs ; he
minds neither Labour, Study nor Prayer ; cafts
away all thoughts of any Thing but the Body belo-
ved ; this is his ftudy, this his moft vain Occupa-

tion. If to Lovers the Succefs be not anfwerable
to their Wifh, or fo foon and profperoufly as they
defire, how many Melancholies hence arife, with
griefs and fadneffes, with which they pine away
and wax fo lean, as they have fcarcely any Flefh clea-
ving to the Bones; yea, at length they loofe the
Life it felf. as may be proved by many Examples!
For fuch Men (which is an horrible thing to think
of) flight and neglect all perils and detriments,
both of the Body and Life, and of the Soul and
Eternal Salvation.

But of thefe enough; for it becomes not a Religious Man to infift too long upon thefe Cogitations, or to give place to fuch a flame in his heart.
Hitherto (without Boafting I fpeak it) I have
throughout the whole courfe of my Life kept my
felf fafe and free from it, and I pray and invoke
G O D to vouchfafe me his Grace, that I may keep
holy and inviolate the Faith, which I have Sworn,
and live contented with my Spiritual Spoufe, the
Holy Catholick Church. For no other Reafon
have I alleaged thefe, then that I might exprefs the
Love, with which all Tinctures ought to be moved toward Metalls, if ever they be admitted by
them into true Friendfhip, and by Love, which penetrates the inmoft parts, be converted into a better State.

Now let us proceed to the Preparation of the
Stone, and leave its ufe to the Clofe of this Difcourfe. This Stone is of a penetrable and fiery
Nature, is cocted and brought to Maturity by fire,
no otherwife, then all other Things, which are
found in this Orb; which notwithftanding as they
are of a divers Nature, fo they in divers man-
ners obtain that, according as the Nature of
Things fupplies with divers Fires.

The firft Fire is *Cœleftial*, by *G O D* kindled in
our

our Hearts, by which being inflamed we are moved
with Love and a certain confidence in and of *G O D*
our Creator, of the Moft Holy and Incomprehenfible *Trinity*, and of the Mercy, Grace of our Saviour
JESUS CHRIST ; which Confidence kin-
dled in Us by Love, never fails, never deferts us in
our Neceffities, but will moft certainly deliver
our Souls from everlafting deftruction.   The fecond Fire is Elemental, produced by the Sun, and
tends to the Ripening of all things in the Macrocofm.   The third Fire is corporal, with which all
Foods and Medicines are cocted and prepared,
without which Men can neither obtain Health of
Body, nor fuftentation of Life.   Of a fourth Fire
mention is made in the Sacred Scriptures, *viz.*
that, which before the Supream Judgment of *G O D*
fhall confume this vifible World : but what Fire is,
and how it fhall operate, that (if we be wife) we
muft leave to be judged of by his own Supream
Majefty.   A fifth Fire is alfo fpoken of in Holy-
Writ, *viz.*   Eternal Fire, in which never to have
end, the Divels fhall never be fet at liberty from
their Infernal Prifon, and wicked Men, their Com-
panions, adjudged to thofe Eternal Fires, fhall be
vexed, punifhed and miferably tormented for ever :
from which I pray the Omnipotent and merciful
Lord to preferve us.   Here I would admonifh all
and every Creature endued with Reafon, by their
Prayers to beg that Grace and Mercy from the Omnipotent, that they may fo conform their Life to
the Divine Precepts, and their own Duty, as that
they may efcape this Fire, and it's Eternal Torments.

Our ftone of Fire (which is to be noted) muft
be cocted and ripened with Corporal Fire in the
Microcofm, as all other Medicines and Foods are
prepared by the fame.   For where the great Fire

of

of the Macrocoſm ceaſeth from it's Operation, there the Microcoſm begins to produce a new Generation; therefore this Concoction ſhould ſeem ſtrange to no Man. Corn is augmented and ripened by the Elementary Fire of the Macrocoſm; but by the Corporal Fire of the Microcoſm a new Coction and maturation is effected, that man may uſe and enjoy that Divine Gift for his ſuſtentation, and by the ſame perfect the Laſt and the Leaſt, which is produced of the Firſt and the Greateſt.

The true Oyl of *Antimony*, of which the ſaid ſtone of Fire is made, is above meaſure ſweet, and from it's earth is in ſuch wiſe purged and ſeparated, as if a Glaſs full of it be expoſed to the Sun, it caſts forth various and wonderful Rays (as if many fiery *Speculums* were there preſent) reſembling a Ruby, and other Colours. Now attend O Lover of Art and Truth, and hear what I ſhall teach.

Take in the Name of the Lord, of the *Minera* of *Antimony*, which grew after the Riſing of the Sun, and Salt Nitre, of each equal Parts; grind them ſubtily and mix them; burn them together with a moderate Fire very artificially and warily; for in this the principal Part of the Work conſiſts. Then you will have a matter inclining to Blackneſs. Of this matter make Glaſs, grind that Glaſs to a ſubtile Pouder, and extract from it an high red Tincture with ſharp diſtilled Vinegar, which is made of it's proper *Minera*. Abſtract the Vinegar in B. M. and a Pouder * will remain, which again extract with Spirit of Wine highly rectifyed, then ſome feces will be put down, and you will have a fair, red, ſweet Extraction, which is of great Uſe in Medicine. This is the pure Sulphur of *Antimony*, which muſt be ſeparated as exactly as is poſſible.

If

If of this Extraction you have ℔. ℥ij. take of the Salt of *Antimony*, as I taught you to prepare it, ℥iiij. and on them pour the Extraction, and circulate them, for a whole Month at leaſt, in a Veſſel well cloſed, and the Salt will unite it ſelf with the Extracted *Sulphur*. If *Fæces* be put down, ſeparate them, and again abſtract the Spirit of Wine by *B. M.* The Pouder which remains urge with vehement Fire, and not without admiration will come forth a varicoloured ſweet Oyl, grateful, pellucid and red. Rectify this Oyl againe in *B. M.* So that a fourth part of it may be diſtilled, and then it is prepared.

This Operation being compleated, take living * *Mercury* of *Antimony*, which I taught you how you ſhould make, and pour

* *The word, Our* Mercury, *which hath ſo often rendred Thee* ambiguous, *is alſo here to be underſtood: for if you take not the true* Mercury *of Philoſophers, you do nothing. Whoſoever he be, that ſhall candidly tell you this, he will be to you* Pylades, *and you to him* Oreſtes, *and nothing will be more pleaſant to me in Life, then to joyn my ſelf to you, as a third Sociate in Friendſhip.*

upon it red Oyl of Vitriol made upon Iron, and highly rectifyed. By Diſtillation in Sand remove the Phlegm from the *Mercury*; then you will have a pretious Precipitate, in Colour ſuch, as never was any more grateful to the Sight; and in Chronical Diſeaſes and open Wounds, it may profitably be uſed for recovering the *priſtine Sanity* For it vehemently dryes up all Symptomatical Humors, whence Martial-Diſeaſes proceed; in which

the

the Spirit of the Oyl, which remains with the *Mercury*, and conjoyns and unites it self thereto, powerfully helps.

Take of this precipitate, and of the Superior Sweet Oyl of *Antimony*, equal parts pour these together into a Phial, which well closed set in convenient heat, and the Precipitate will in time resolve and fix it self in the Oyl. Also the Phlegm by the Fire will be consumed, and what remains become a Red, dry, fixed and fluid * Pouder which will not in the least give forth from it self any Fume.

* *Far hence, far hence ye Prophane, and you that are initiated in the Sacred Mysteries of Chymistry keep silence. Let the King enter into his Bed-Chamber, that he may consummate his Marriage.*

O tua te quantis attollet Gloria rebus,
Connubio tali ! ————————

Yet make not too much haste to enter, or disturb this Matrimonial Conjunction, let them for many Months delight themselves with their mutual Embraces, and not go forth, until from their mutual Love they be changed into an Hermaphroditick Body, and have produced that Son desired by all, if not a King of Kings, yet at least a Regulus or Ruler, which delivers his Subjects from Diseases and Necessity.

Now my Follower. and Disciple of Arcanums, I will speak after a Prophetick manner. When you have brought your Philosophick Studies (in the Method by me prescribed) to this end, you have the Medicine of Men and Metals; which is grateful and Sweet in use, without all peril, it is penetrative, yet causeth not Stools, it induceth Emendation, and expells Evil. Use it as is fit; and it will yeild you many Commodities, both for health, and temporal necessity; by which means you will be freed from want in this World; which is a thing of so great Moment, as no Sacrifice of Gratitude

titude can be found sufficient to answer this favour of *G O D* shewed to you.

Here, O my *G O D*, I as a Religious Man am troubled in Mind; and know not whether I do well or ill, whether in * speaking I have exceeded or not reached the due Bounds; whilst I propose, and shew to every One, as it were, his proper House. Do thou, that art a young Follower of Art, inquire, search and try, as I have done; if you attain your End, give greatest thanks to *G O D*, and after him to me your Master. But if you turn aside into devious and by-paths, blame your self, not me; for I am not guilty of your Error.

* *Our Author judgeth himself to have spoken too much, if you also think the same, you will rejoyce in his Sadness. Yet it is strange, that no Man can contribute a little Light to this Philosophy, but he presently repents.*

Now I have said enough, and writ enough, and taught so clearly and openly, and plainly, as more manifestly or clearly cannot be done by Writing, unless some lost and rash Man, knowing and willingly would cast himself into Hell, to be there Submerged and Perish: Because, by the Creator of all Things we are most severely prohibited further to unlock these Mysteries, or to eat of the Tree which was planted in the midst of Paradise. Therefore here I will desist, until Others shew, what is here to be done by Me, and what they judge is to be omitted, and say no more of this, but pass to its Use.

Therefore know, that the Use consists in Observation of the Person and his Complexion, with relation to what appertains to Humane Health, that Nature be not overpowered with two great a Quantity, or not helped by too small. Yet too much is not so Religiously to be feared; for it will not readily

readily hurt;becaufe it helps to recover the priftine
Sanity, and fights againft Venom, if any be in
the Body: This I only add, three or four grains
of it, given in one onely Dofe, are fufficient for
evpelling every Evil, if taken in Spirit of Wine.'
For this Stone or Tincture paffeth through all the
Members of the Body, and contains in it felf the
Virtues of many *Arcanums*. It remedies the Gid-
dinefs of the Head, and all Difeafes, which have
their Original from the Lungs. It cures difficulty of Breathing, and the Cough ; the Leprofy and
French Difeafe are amended by it, in a wonderful
manner. The Peft, Jaundies, Dropfies and all
kinds of Fevers, are often cured by it, Likewife
it expells Venom taken. It profits thofe, who
have drunk a *Philtrum* or Love-potion: it confirms all the Members, Brain, Head, and all things
depending thereon. It helps the Stomach and Liver; heals all Difeafes, which proceed from the
Reins ; cleanfeth the impurity of the Bloud. Alfo
this Tincture of *Antimony*, breaks the Stone of
the Bladder to Pouder ; and expells it; it provokes
Urine, when ftopped by *Flatus's*. It reftores the
vital Spirits, cures Suffocation of the Matrix, makes
the Menftrues flow if ftopped, and ftayes them if
inordinate. It caufeth Fruitfulnefs, and makes the
Seed found, and avaylable for Generation, both in
Women and Men. Laftly, this Stone of Fire inwardly taken (convenient Plaifters being alfo
outwardly applyed) heals the Cancer, Fiftula's,
Rottenefs in the Bones, and all corroding Ulcers,
and whatfoever takes beginning from the Impurity of the Blood, alfo the Difeafe it felf called *Noli
me tangere*. And that I may comprehend all in few
Words, this Stone, like a Particular Tincture, is a
* Remedy againft all Symptomes, which can happen to the Humane Body. All which Experience
                                                will

will very clearly demonstrate to you, and open the way further to you, if you be a Physitian, called by *G O D* to that Office.

* Here the Medicinal Virtues are spoken of at large. For Basilius supposeth Thee not to be defiled with the Filths of Avarice, but splendid in the Light of Charity, and burning with a Desire of helping thy Neighbour, following him discovering these Secrets. Now farewel O Lover of Chymistry, and if thou, hast gained any Light, either from the Interpretation of Basilius, or my Commentaries, enjoy it, and communicate the same to the Sons of Art, that Philosophy oppressed for so many Years with the intollerable Yoak of Avarice, may at length be revived, and a return be of those times of the Egyptians, in which Trismegistus and so many wise Magi, Philosophized not with empty denominations, but with wonderful Works.

In these, I think I have done my part, and writ more then sufficiently of *Antimony.* If any One followes me, he may add his own Experiences to these, that (with the singular favour of *G O D*) before the consummation of the World, the Mysteries of the most High may be revealed, to his Glory and honour, and the Conservation of health. Having finished this Discourse, I intend for a time to be silent and return to my Monastery, there to learn Philosophy further, that I may be able to comment of other Things and as I have already promised, I shall (*G O D* willing) write of Vitriol, common Sulphur, and the Loadstone, and open their Principle, Powers, Operations and Virtues.

Let G O D *the Lord of Heaven and Earth grant to us temporal Health here, and hereafter Eternal Salvation for the Refreshment of our Souls, in the Seats of Joy and Gladness, never to be limited within any Bounds of time. Amen.*

Thus I conclude this Treatise of *Antimony,* and all whatsoever I have written of the Red Oyl of *Antimony,* which is made of its Sulphur highly purified, and of the Spirit, which is prepared of its Salt.

Incline

Incline your Mind to thoſe, and with them compare theſe laſt, which I have preſcribed you touching the Stone of Fire. If you acutely conſider them, you may eaſily find their Union unto the End, by this Comparation. For the Foundation is the ſame, the Reaſon the ſame, the Friendſhip the ſame, by which Health is required, and the Stag long ſought taken with a pleaſant Hunting.

FINIS.

THE
TRUE BOOK
Of the Learned
SYNESIUS
A
Greek Abbot,
Taken out of the
EMPEROUR'S LIBRARY,
Concerning the
Philofopher's Stone.

Homer.

Hæc partim ipfe tuo perpendens pectore tecum,
Partim Divum aliquis tibi fuggerat.——

To fo great a Myftery who fhall Afpire.

London, Printed for *Dorman Newman* at the Kings Arms
in the *Poultry*. 1678.

THE
TRUE BOOK

of the Learned Greek Abbot

SYNESIUS

TAKEN OUT OF THE

Emperours' Library.

Though the Antient Philofophers have written diverfly of this fcience, con-cealing under a multitude of names the true principles of the Art; yet have they not done it but upon important confiderati-ons as we fhall hereafter make appear. And though they are different in their expreffions, yet are they not any way difcordant one from another, but ayming all at one end, and fpeaking of the fame thing, they have thought fit (above all the reft) to name the *proper Agent*, by a term, ftrange, nay fometimes contrary to its nature and qualities.

Know then, my Son, that almighty God toge-ther with this Univerfe, created two *Stones*, that is to fay, the *White* and the *Red*, both which are un-

M 2   der

der one and the same subject, and afterwards mul-
tiplied in such abundance, that every one may take
as much as he please thereof. The matter of them
is of such a kind, that it seems to be a mean between
Metal and *Mercury*, and is partly fixed and partly
not fixed, otherwise it could not be a mean be-
twixt *Metalls* and *Mercury* : and this matter is the
instrument whereby our desire is accomplished, if
we do but prepare it. Hence it comes that those
who bestow their endeavours in this Art without
the said *medium*, loose their labour, but if they are
acquainted with the *Medium*, they shall find all
things feasible and fortunate. Know then that
this *Medium*, being aerial, is found among the ce-
lestial Bodies, and that it is onely there are found
the Masculine and Feminine Gender, (to speak
properly) having a constant, strong, fixed and
permanent Virtue, of the essence whereof (as I have
told thee) Philosophers have expressed themselves
only by Similitudes and Figures. This they did,
that the science might not be discovered by the
Ignorant, which if it should once happen, all were
lost : but that it might be comprehended only by
those patient souls, and subtilized understandings,
which being sequestred from the sovlines of this
world, are cleansed from the filth of that terrene
dunghil of Avarice, whereby the ignorant are
chained to the earthines of this World, which is
(without this admirable quintessence) the recep-
tacle of poverty; it being certain, that those divine souls, when they have div'd into *Democritus's*
Fountain, that is to say, into the truth of Nature,
would soon discover what confusion might happen
in all estates and conditions, if every one could
make as much Gold as he would himself. Upon
this ground was it that they were pleased to speak
by figures, types, and analogies, that so they might
not

not be underftood but by fuch as are difcreet, religious, and enlightned by (divine) Wifdome.
All which notwithftanding, they have left in their
writings a certain method, way and rule, by the
affiftance whereof the wife man may comprehend
whatever they have written moft obfcurely, and
in time arrive at the knowledge of it, though haply
wading through fome error, as I have done,praifed
be God for it.   And whereas the Vulgar ignorant
perfon ought to fubmit to thefe reafons, and confequently adore, what is too great, to enter into his
Brain, he on the contrary accufes the Philofophers
of impofture and impiety, by which means, and the
fcarcity of wife men, the Art falls into contempt.

But for my part, I tell ›thee, they have always
expreffed themfelves according to certain Truth,
though very obfcurely, and fometimes fabuloufly,
all which I have difcipher'd in this little Treatife,and
that after fuch a manner that the earneft defirer of
Science fhall underftand what hath been myftically
delivered by the Philofophers.   And yet if he pre-
tend to underftand me and know not the nature of
the Elements and things created, as alfo our rich
Metal, he doth but lofe his Labour : but if he underftand the Concord and Difcord of Natures, he
will by God's affiftance arrive to the reft ? It is
therefore my fuit to God, that he who fhall underftand the prefent Secret may work to the glory and
praife of the facred Divinity.

Know then my dear Son, that the ignorant man
cannot comprehend the fecret of the Art, becaufe
it depends upon the Knowledge of the true Body,
which is hidden from him.   Know then, my Son,
pure and *impure*, the *clean* and *unclean* Natures, for
there cannot come from any thing that which it
hath not. For things, that are not or have not, cannot give but their own Nature: make ufe then of

that

that which is moſt perfect and neareſt in kind,
thou ſhalt meet with, and it ſhall ſuffice.   Avoid
then that which is *mixt*, and take the *ſimple*, for that
proceeds from the *Quinteſſence*.   Note that we
have two bodies of very great perfection, full of
Mercury : Out of theſe extract thy *Mercury*, and of
that thou ſhalt make the *Medicine*, called by ſome
Quinteſſence, which is a Vertue or power that is im-
periſhable, permanent, and perpetually victorious,
nay it is a clear Light, which ſheds true goodneſs
into every ſoul that hath once taſted of it.   It is
the knot and link of all the Elements, which it contains in it ſelf, as being alſo the Spirit which nou-
riſheth all things, and by the aſſiſtance whereof Nature works in the Univerſe.   It is the force, the
beginning and end of the whole work, and to lay
all open to thee in a word, know, that the *Quinteſ-
fence* and the hidden thing of our Stone is nothing
elſe then our viſcous, celeſtial and glorious Soul
drawn by our Magiſtery out of its Mine, which engenders it ſelf, and that it is not poſſible for us to
make that water by Art, but Nature alone begets it,
and that water is the *moſt ſharp Vinegar*, which makes
Gold to be a pure ſpirit, nay it is that *bleſſed Nature*
which engenders all things, which through its putrefaction is become a Tri-unity, and by reaſon of
its Viridity cauſes an appearance of divers colours.
And I adviſe thee, my Son, make no account of any
other things, (as being vain,) labour only for that
water, which *burns to blackneſs , whitens, diſſolves* and
congeals.   It is that which putrefies, and cauſes
germination, and therefore I adviſe thee, that thou
wholly imploy thy ſelf in the decoction of this
water, and quarrel not at the expence of time, o-
therwiſe thou ſhalt have no advantage.   Decoct it
gently by little and little, until it have changed its
falſe colour into a perfect, and have a great care at
the

the beginning that thou burn not its Flowers and
its vivacity, and make not too much haft to come to
an end of thy work. Shut thy Veffel well, that
what is within may not breath out, and fo thou mayft
bring it to fome effect. And note, that to *diffolve*,
to *calcine*, to *tinge*, to *whiten*, to *renew*, to *bath*, to
wafh, to *coagulate*, to *imbibe*, to *decoct*, to *fix*, to *grind*,
to *dry*; and to *diftil*, are all one, and fignify no more
then to *concoct* Nature, until fuch time as it be perfect. Note further that to extract the foul, or
the fpirit, or the body, is nothing elfe then the
abovefaid Calcinations, in regard they fignify the
operation of *Venus*. It is therefore through the
fire of the extraction of the foul that the fpirit
comes forth gently, underftand me. The fame
may alfo be faid of the extraction of the foul out of
the Body, and the reduction of it afterwards upon
the fame Body, until the whole be drawn to a commixtion of all the four Elements. And fo that
which is below, is like that which is above, and
confequently there are made therein two lumina-
ries, the one fixt the other not, whereof the fix'd
remains below, and the volatile above, moving it
felf perpetually, until that which is below, which is
the male, get upon the female, and all be fixed, and
then iffues out an incomparable Luminary. And
as in the beginning, there was onely one, fo in this
Matter, all proceeds from one and returns to one,
which is called a converfion of the Elements, and
to convert the Elements, is as much as to make the
humid dry, and the volatile fixed, that fo that
which is thick may be made thin, and weaken the
thing that fixeth the reft, the fixative part of the
thing remaining intire. Thus happens the life and
death of the Elements, which compofed germinate
and produce, and fo one thing perfects another,
and affifts it to oppofe the Fire.

The Practice.

MY Son it is neceſſary that thou work with the *Mercury of the Philoſophers* and the wiſe, which is not the *Vulgar*, nor hath any thing of the *Vulgar*, but, according to them, is the *firſt Matter*, the *Soul of the World*, the cold *Element*, the *bleſſed Water*, *the Water of the Wiſe*, the *Venemous Water*, the *moſt ſharp Vinegar*, the *Mineral Water*, the *Water of celeſtial grace*, the *Virgin Milk*, our *Mineral and corporeal Mercury*. For this alone perfects both the ſtones, the *White* and the *Red*. Conſider what *Geber* ſayes, that our Art conſiſts not in the multitude of ſeveral things, becauſe the *Mercury* is but one only thing, that is to ſay, one only Stone wherein conſiſts the whole Magiſtery; to which thou ſhalt not add any ſtrange thing, ſave that in the preparation thereof thou ſhalt take away from it whatſoever is ſuperfluous, by reaſon that in this matter, all things requiſite to this Art are contained. And therefore it is very obſervable that he ſaies, we muſt add nothing that is ſtrange, ſave the Sun and Moon for the red and white Tincture, which are not ſtrange [to it] but are its Ferment, by which the work is accompliſhed. Laſtly, mark my Son, that theſe Suns and Moons are not the ſame with the Vulgar Gold and Silver, for that our Suns and Moons are better in their nature then the Vulgar Suns and Moons. For our Suns and Moons are in their nature living, and thoſe of the Vulgar are dead in compariſon of ours, which are exiſtent and permanent in our Stone. Whence thou maiſt obſerve that the Mercury drawn out of our Bodies, is like the aqueous and common Mercury, and for that reaſon, enjoyes it ſelf and takes pleaſure in its like, and is more glad

of

of its company, as it happens in the fimple and compound, which thing hath not been difcovered by the Philofophers in their Books.And the advantage therefore which is in this Art, lies in the Mercury, Sun and Moon. *Diomedes* faith, make ufe of fuch a matter as to which thou muft not introduce any ftrange thing, neither pouder nor water, for that feveral things do not improve our Stone, and thereby he fufficiently inftructs him, who underftands him, that the tincture of our Stone is not drawn from any thing but the Mercury of the Philofophers; which is their principle, their root, and their great Tree, fprouting forth into boughs and branches.

The firft Operation,

SUBLIMATION·

IT is not Vulgar but Philofophical whereby we take away from the Stone whatever is fuperfluous, which, in effect is nothing elfe, but the elevation of the not-fixed part by fume and vapor, for the fixed part fhould remain in the bottom, nor would we that one fhould be feparated from the other, but that they remain and be fixed together. Know alfo that he, who fhall fublime our Philofophical Mercury (wherein is all the vertue of our Stone) as it ought to be done, fhall perfect the Magiftery. This gave *Geber* reafon to fay that all perfection confifts in *Sublimation*, and in this Sublimation all other operations, that is to fay, *Diftillation,*

*tion, Affation, Destruction, Coagulation, Putrefaction,
Calcination, Fixation, Reduction* of *the White and Red
Tinctures,* procreated and engendred in one furnace
and in one Veſſel, and this is the ready way to the
final Conſummation, whereof the Philoſophers
have made divers chapters, purpoſely to amuſe the
Ignorant.

Take then in the name of the great God, the
venerable matter of the Philoſophers, called the
firſt *Hyle* of the Sages, which contains the above named Philoſophical Mercury, termed, the firſt matter of the perfect Body, put it into its Veſſel, which
muſt be clear, diaphanous and round, and cloſely
ſtopped by the *Seal of Seals,* and make it hot in its
place, well prepared, with temperate heat, for the
ſpace of a *Philoſophical Month,* keeping it ſix weeks
and two days in the ſweat of Sublimation until it begins to be putrefyed, to ferment, to be coloured
and to be congealed with its metallick humidity,
and be fixed ſo far, that it do no more aſcend in
aiery fumous ſubſtance, but remain fixed in the bottom, turned from what it was, and deveſted of all
viſcous humidity, putrefyed and black, which is called the ſable Robe, Night or the Crowes-head.
Thus when our ſtone is in the veſſel, and that it
mounts up on high in fume, this is called *Sublimation,* and when it falls down from on high, *Diſtillation,* and *Deſcenſion.* When it begins to participate of the fumous ſubſtance, and to be putrefyed,
and that by reaſon of the frequent aſcent and de-
ſcent it begins to coagulate, then it is *Putrefaction*
and devouring Sulphur, and laſtly through the
want or privation of the humidity of the radical
water is wrought *Calcination* and *Fixation* both at the
ſame time, by decoction alone, in one onely Veſſel,
as I have already ſaid. Moreover in this ſublimation is wrought the true ſeparation of the Elements,
for

for in our Sublimation the *Elixir* is turned from
Water into a terreſtrial Element dry and hot, by
which operation it is manifeſt, that the ſeparation
of the four Elements in our Stone is not Vulgar but
Philoſophical. Hence alſo is it, that in our Stone
there are but two *formal* Elements, that is to ſay,
Earth and Water; but the Earth hath in its groſ-
neſs, the virtue and drought of Fire; and the Water contains in it ſelf the air with its humidity.
Thus we have in our Stone viſibly but two elements,
but effectually there are four. And by this thou
maiſt judge, that the ſeparation of the four Elements is abſolutely phyſical not vulgar and real,
ſuch as the ignorant daily employ themſelves in.
Continue therefore its decoction with a gentle
fire, until all the black matter appearing in the ſu-
perficies be quite diſſipated by the Magiſtery, which
blackneſs is by the Philoſophers called the dark
mantle of the Stone, which afterwards becoming
clear is termed the cleanſing water of the earth, or
rather the Elixir. And note, that the blackneſs which
appears is a ſign of putrefaction. And the beginning of the diſſolution is a ſign of the conjunction
of both Natures. And this blackneſs appears ſometimes in forty dayes, more or leſs, according to the
quantity of the matter, and the induſtry of the
Operator, which contribntes much to the ſeparation of the ſaid Blackneſs. Now my Son, by the
grace of God thou art acquainted with one Element
of our Stone, which is the black earth, the Ravens
head, by ſome called the obſcure ſhadow, upon
which earth as upon a baſe all the reſt is grounded.
This terreſtial and dry Element, is called, *Laton*,
the *Bull, black Dregs, our Metall, our Mercury*. And
thus by the privation of the aduſt humidity, which
is taken away by Philoſophical ſublimation, the volatile is fixed, and the moiſt is made dry and earth;
nay,

nay, according to *Geber*, there is wrought a change of the complexion, as of a cold and humid Nature, into dry choler; and according to *Alphidius*, of a liquid into a thick. Whence is apprehended what the Philosophers mean when they say, that the operation of our Stone is only a transmutation of Nature and a revolution of Elements. Thou seeft then how that by this incorporation the humid becomes dry, the volatile fixed, the Spiritual corporeal, the liquid thick, water fire, air earth, and that there happens an infallible change in their true nature, and a certain circulation of the four Elements.

The second Operation,

DEALBATION.

IT converts our *Mercury* into the *white* Stone, and that by decoction only. When the earth is separated from its water, then must the Vessel be set on the Ashes, as is usual in a distilling furnace, and the water be distilled by a gentle fire at the beginning, so that the water come so gently that thou mayst distinctly number as far as forty names, or pronounce fifty six words, and let this order be observed in all the distillations of the black earth, and that which is in the bottom of the Vessel, that is, the *Fæces* remaining to be imbibed, with the new water, will be dissolved, which water will contain three or four parts more then those *Fæces*, that so all may be dissolved and converted into Mercury and *Argent vive*. I tell thee that this must be done so often, that

there

there shall remain nothing but the Murc. For this distillation there is no time limited, but it is done sooner or later according to the greater or lesser quantity of the water, proportionably to the quantity of the fire. Then take the earth which thou shalt have reserved in a Vessel of Glass, with its distilled water, and with a soft and gentle fire, such as was that of Distillation, or purification, or rather one somewhat stronger, continue it, till such time as the earth be dry and white, and by reason of its drought, drunk up all its water. This done, put to it some of the abovesaid water, and so, as at the beginning, continue on the same decoction, until that earth is become absolutely white, cleansed and clear, and have drunk all its water. And note that the said earth will be washed from its blackness by the decoction, as I have said, because it is easily putrefyed by its own water, and is cleansed, which is the end of the Magistery, and then be sure to keep that white earth very carefully. For that is the *White Mercury, White Magnesia, Foliated earth.* Then take this white earth rectified as abovesaid, and put it into its vessel upon the ashes, to a fire of Sublimation, and let it have a very strong fire until all the coagulated water, which is within, come into the Alembick, and the earth remain in the bottom well calcined: then hast thou the earth, the water, and the air, and though the earth have in it the nature of the fire, yet is it not apparent in effect, as thou shalt see, when by a greater decoction thou shalt make it become red; so that then thou shalt manifestly see the fire in appearance, and such must be the proceeding in order to Fermentation of the white earth, that the dead body may be animated and enlivened, and its vertue be multiplyed to infinity. But note, that the Ferment cannot enter into the dead body, but by the means of the water,

which

which hath made a contract and a marriage between the Ferment and the white earth. And know that in all Fermentation the weight is to be confidered, that fo the quantity of the volatile exceed not the fixed, and that the marriage pafs away in fume. For, as *Senior* fayes, if thou convert not the earth into water, and the water into fire, there cannot be a conjunction of the fpirit and body. To do this take a *Lamen* or plate red hot and caft on it a drop of our Medicine, which penetrating, it fhall be of a perfect colour, and will be a fign of perfection. If it happen it do not tinge, reiterate the diffolution and coagulation, until it do tinge and penetrate. And note, that feven imbibitions, at the moft, are fufficient, and five at the leaft, that fo the matter may be liquifyed, and without fmoak, and then the matter is perfect as to whitenefs, for as much as the matter fometimes requires a longer time to be fixed, and fometimes is done in a fhortèr, according to the quantity of the Medicine. And note that our Medicine from the creation of our Mercury requires the term of feven months to compafs the whitenefs, and, to arrive at the rednefs, five; which put together, make twelve.

Of the third Operation,

RUBIFICATION.

TAke of the white Medicine, as much as thou wilt, and put it with its Glafs upon the hot afhes, till it becomes as dry as the afhes. Then put to it fome water of the Sun, which thou haft

kept purpofely for that end, and continue the fire
to the fecond degree, until it become dry, then put
to it again fome of the abovefaid water, and fo fuc-
ceffively imbibe and dry, until the matter be rubi-
fied, and fluxible as wax, and cover with it the red
Lamen, as hath been faid, and the matter fhall be
perfect as to *rednefs*. But note that at every time,
thou needft put no more of the water of the Sun
then is barely neceffary to cover the body, and this
is done that the Elixir fink not and be drowned,
and fo the fire muft be continued unto deficcation,
and then muft there be made a fecond imbibition,
and fo proceed in order to the perfection of the
Medicine, that is to fay, until the force of the digeftion of the fire convert it into a very red pouder, which is the *true Hyle* of the Philofophers, the
bloody Stone, the purple red Coral, the pretious
Ruby, red Mercury and the red Tincture.

PROJECTION.

THe oftner thou fhalt diffolve and coagulate it,
the more will the Vertue of it be multiplyed
to infinity. But note that the medicine is multiplyed later by *Solution*, then by *Fermentation*.
Wherefore the thing diffolved operates not well, if
it be not before fixed in its ferment. Neverthelefs
the multiplication of the Medicine by folution
is more abondant then that of the Ferment, by reafon there is more fubtilization. Yet I advife
thee that in the multiplication thou put one part
of the work upon four of the other, and in a fhort
time there will be made a pouder, all Ferment,

The

The Epilogue according to
HERMES.

THus art thou to feparate the *earth* from the *fire*, the *grofs* from the *fubtil* gently, with great Judgment, that is to fay, feparate the parts that are united to the Furnace, by the diffolution and feparation of the parts, as the earth from the fire, the fubtile from the grofs, &c. that is to fay, the more pure fubftance of the ftone, until thou haft got it clean, and free from all fpots or filth. And when he faith, *it afcends from the earth up into Heaven and returns again into the earth*, there is no more to be underftood by it then the *Sublimation* of the Bodies. Further, to explain what diftillation is, he fayes *the Wind carryes it in its belly*, that is, when the water is diftilled by the Alembick, where it firft afcends by a wind full of Fume and Vapour, and afterwards returns to the bottom of the Veffel in water again. When he would alfo exprefs the congelation of the matter, he fayes, *Its force is abfolute, if it be turned into earth*, that is to fay, be converted by decoction. And to make a general demonftration of all hath been faid, he fayes, *It fhall receive both the inferior and fuperior force*, that is to fay, that of the Elements, for as much as, if the Medicine receive the force of the lighter parts, that is to fay, air and fire, it fhall alfo receive that of the more grave and weighty parts, changing it felf into water and earth, to the end, that the Matters being thus perpetually joined together, may have permanence, durance, conftancy, and ftability. Glory be to God.